Living in the Shadows

Anti-colonial Educational Perspectives for Transformative Change

Executive Series Editor

Pierre Wilbert Orelus (*Fairfield University, CT, USA*)

Executive Board Members

Antonia Darder (*LMU, School of Education, LA, USA*)
George Sefa Dei (*University of Toronto, Canada*)
Venus Evans-Winters (*Illinois State University, USA*)
Curry Malott (*West Chester University of Pennsylvania, West Chester, PA, USA*)
Peter Mayo (*University of Malta, Malta*)
Peter McLaren (*UCLA, CA, USA*)
Binaya Subedi (*Ohio State University, OH, USA*)

VOLUME 9

The titles published in this series are listed at *brill.com/acep*

Living in the Shadows

A Biographical Account of Racial, Class, and Gender Inequities in the Americas

By

Pierre W. Orelus

BRILL
SENSE

LEIDEN | BOSTON

All chapters in this book have undergone peer review.

The Library of Congress Cataloging-in-Publication Data is available online at http://catalog.loc.gov

Typeface for the Latin, Greek, and Cyrillic scripts: "Brill". See and download: brill.com/brill-typeface.

ISSN 2542-9280
ISBN 978-90-04-43080-8 (paperback)
ISBN 978-90-04-43081-5 (hardback)
ISBN 978-90-04-44094-4 (e-book)

Copyright 2020 by Pierre W. Orelus. Published by Koninklijke Brill NV, Leiden, The Netherlands. Koninklijke Brill NV incorporates the imprints Brill, Brill Hes & De Graaf, Brill Nijhoff, Brill Rodopi, Brill Sense, Hotei Publishing, mentis Verlag, Verlag Ferdinand Schöningh and Wilhelm Fink Verlag. Koninklijke Brill NV reserves the right to protect this publication against unauthorized use. Requests for re-use and/or translations must be addressed to Koninklijke Brill NV via brill.com or copyright.com.

This book is printed on acid-free paper and produced in a sustainable manner.

Advance Praise for
Living in the Shadows: A Biographical Account of Racial, Class, and Gender Inequities in the Americas

"Tracing his intellectual development from childhood in Port-au-Prince to adulthood in Massachusetts and thereafter, Pierre Orelus provides an historical account of self that is sure to haunt us. Despite ascending the U.S. class ladder through education, Orelus runs into the fact of race to remind us that the coloniality of whiteness in 'America' places limitations on black intellectuals. In this gripping, reflective narrative, Orelus lets us in to the trauma-inducing experience of striving, while surviving, under white supremacy. It engages the intellect simultaneously with intense emotion, quiet rage, and a sense of hope in the struggle for personhood. At once personal and analytical, *Living in the Shadows* is critical scholarship in the most meaningful sense of that phrase." – **Zeus Leonardo, Professor and Associate Dean, Graduate School of Education and Faculty of the Critical Theory Designated Emphasis, University of California, Berkeley, author of *Edward Said and Education***

"With uninhibited honesty and detail, Dr. Pierre Orelus takes us through his struggles and consternations. His is a story that is not fearful of contradictions, but is instead one that is willing to push the work forward in a place that was never meant for us. I am humbled by his candor and encouraged by his willingness to challenge notions of 'success' in the hallowed halls of academe." – **David Stovall, PhD, University of Illinois at Chicago**

"In this book, Dr. Orelus writes a deeply personal story that addresses some of the childhood trauma as a child growing up in Haiti who immigrated to the United States as a college student. He went to complete a doctorate and became a successful scholar. As he tells his life story, he also elucidates how both oppression and privilege shaped his life experience. His reflection on his own positionality further strengthens his strong critique of the ways in which BIPOC scholars in the academy are treated. His accounts of being racially profiled in multiple contexts in the US – both on and off-campus – give readers incredible insight into what Black scholars experience before they enter the classroom. BIPOC scholars' experiences within the halls of the academy are equally problematic. Dr. Orelus's work is significant because it gives it clear insights into the experiences of Black immigrants in the US while also shedding significant light on what universities must do in order to create more inclusive communities for BIPOC scholars." – **Marvin Lynn, PhD, Dean & Professor, College of Education, Portland State University**

To my Afro-Caribbean mother, Leanne Adelson (Daya),
who never stops fighting for her human dignity and respect.

May you continue to live, mama!

∴

Contents

Foreword   XI
Peter Mayo
Preface   XIV
Acknowledgements   XVII

Introduction   1
1   Overview of the Book   3
2   Conclusion   4

1   Home and Early Literacy Memories   5
1   Recollect My Childhood and Adolescence Memories   5
2   Early Literacy   7
3   Attending School in the Countryside   9
4   Gender Inequities   14

2   Questioning My Black Male and Heterosexual Privileges   20
1   Teenage and Young Adult Life Remembrances   20
2   Critical Reflection   29

3   Growing up Poor and Black and Succeeding in an Uneven World   31
1   My *Mis-Education*   36
2   Conclusion   39

4   Belonging Neither Here nor There   40
1   I Am My Identities   40
2   Recollecting Precious Memories   42
3   Coping with Bitter and Sweet Feelings Living in the United States   44
4   Awareness as Liberation   46
5   Conclusion   52

5   To Be Non-White in America Is to Be in Danger   53
1   Perceived and Treated as a Problem in America   54
2   Experiencing Inequities in the Main Land   56

6   Succeeding as Black in an Uneven Western World   60
1   Challenges   60
2   Confronting Linguistic and Racial Discrimination   61
3   Lessons Learned from My Personal Journey   65

CONTENTS

7 **What It Means Being Black in the Ivy Halls of White America** 67
  1 Longing for a Paradigm Shift: Will That Ever Occur? 70
  2 Teaching While Black: Confronting Whiteness in the Classroom 75
  3 The Inner Fear of Losing Myself 81
  4 Conclusion 86

8 **The Cost of Being Black and Brown Laboring in Predominantly White Institutions** 88
  1 Going through the Hoops of the Tenure and Promotion Process 89
  2 Post-Tenure and Promotion Critical Self-Reflection 94
  3 Looking Forward 96

Afterword 98
  Peter McLaren

References 101

Foreword

Like many others, I have followed attentively and painfully recent events marking the fall-out from the callous murder of George Floyd perpetrated by insensitive members of the US repressive state apparatus. I had been filled with revulsion and indignation at news and footage of the act. This is the latest in a series of acts of violence against African-Americans harkening back to slavery and its aftermath, the Jim Crow laws, subsequent murders (lynching etc.) and humiliation of Black people in the US. Quite recently, as I write, we commemorated the 50th anniversary of the shooting and killing of Black students in Jackson State. These remembrances provide an opportunity to reflect on racism, and Identity issues more generally, throughout the world and especially within both sides of the constructed 'North' and 'South' divide.

Pierre Orelus' book, couched in an autobiographical, reflective idiom, can have a cathartic effect on us. The issues involved make their presence felt in our own life as people located differentially and hopefully as 'persons in process'.

My own country, the island of Malta, located in close proximity to Tunisia on one side and Sicily on the other, alas has not been immune to cases of overt violence, in addition to many forms of symbolic violence, against Black people in a variety of places. They sometimes result in the killing of innocent people ostensibly because of 'public disturbance' but more likely because of cases of white or 'shades of white' supremacy over and antipathy towards people of a particular skin colour.

All this culminated in the wanton killing of Lassana Cisse, originally from the Côte d'Ivoire, for the alleged sport of people belonging to the country's Armed Forces. The very same people who are meant to protect human beings from incidents of racism were, just over one year ago, the alleged perpetrators of this very same racist murderous act. This act reflects the warped mind-set which regards 'white supremacy' as the norm and certain people, as, in Edward Said's expression, "lesser beings."

Pierre Orelus' autobiographical book can help us understand the kind of environment that breeds such hatred in Western countries, such as the most Western of the West context to which he moved from one of the, alas, poorest per capita nations, Haiti. The new country of his residence provides, in its various subtle and not so subtle forms of white supremacy, a fertile ground for calamitous manifestations of racial abuse and suffering. They have, alas, been the staple of race relations in this state since its inception predicated on Indigenous subjugation, cleansing and a global slave trade. This is the country where Pierre, significantly hailing from Haiti, took up the academic life with its mirroring of many of the tensions and aggressions that abound throughout US society in general.

The occurrences range from forms of micro-aggressions, reflected in stereotyping and self-fulfilling prophecies, to overt violence, constant security threats to and deaths of Black people in the US and other parts of the world (e.g. Indigenous people in Brasil). Yet, as Pierre Orelus shows, racism intersects with other aggressions, micro or macro, of which the author was both victim and perpetrator, something he struggled against as a 'person in process', unlearning social class (a male professor), gender and heteronormative privilege. The light he sheds on how these intersections occur, in the spirit of Kimberlé W. Crenshaw's notion of 'intersectionality', is one of the strengths of this book. The author, as subject-to-think-with, is at pains to present himself not simply as victim but also as indirect agent (as many of us are in our not overt but unintended aggressions) in this unfairly differentiated world socially constructed. Ongoing praxis in which one can struggle to become less unfinished, less incomplete, in Paulo Freire's immortal words, is the leitmotif of this autobiographical account. It is an account which reflects the length to which highly 'educated' people can go, in say academia, to give vent to their deep-seated antagonistic dispositions towards those they construct, despite much evidence to the contrary, as "lesser beings" in the so-called land of the free – free in a Darwinian sense. The bourgeois white 'toothpaste smile' world of polite 'conversations', rather than confrontations of ideas, rigidly policed bodies, as opposed to movement throughout the flesh (social class and ethnic markers), and tone of voice, drab appeasing monotones as opposed to richer, more expressive and evocative tones reminiscent of a Paul Robeson or Angela Davis, are the order of the day. Different forms of racial and social class aggressions can occur in each case. 'Being vocal' is the expression I recall from my brief stints living in North America.

And yet, as Antonio Gramsci instructs us, one cannot really understand the different worlds of migrants, unless one understands the origins in the country they or their parents or ancestors left to take up residence elsewhere. Only thus can one understand how 'Haitians,' 'South-East Asians,' 'Africans,' 'Italians' and others are, despite some commonalities as a group, differentially located through different variables. One therefore needs to know the context of origin and their discursive location within them to be able to understand them or their progeny in their present country of abode.

This book does not disappoint in this regard. It, to the contrary, provides much grist for the mill. The author's two worlds of Haiti and the USA are juxtaposed. Haiti, ancestral home of W.E.B. Dubois, is presented as a place where 'race' and ethnicity were more of a collective issue than a source of individual differentiation. The differentiation occurred more as a result of intersections with social class, gender, ability and sexual orientation.

As for the USA, 'race', crisscrossed by social class, is, to state the obvious, a key source of differentiating politics and life-chances. In *Living in the Shadows: A Biographical Account of Racial, Class and Gender Inequalities in the Americas*, Pierre Orelus illuminated these differences in the everyday life of individuals straddling these two contexts. For Black people such as Pierre, these differences can prove to be a matter of life and death, as the Floyd-style murders by US policemen and the drive-by shooting, for sport, of Lassana by two members of the Maltese Armed Forces, show us only too well.

Peter Mayo
University of Malta

Preface

After I graduated from high school and attended college for about two years in Haiti, I immigrated to the United States. When I arrived here, I attended a community college while at the same time taking basic ESL classes at a community center in Cambridge, Massachusetts, at night to improve my English speaking, reading and writing skills. While I was a student there, I met a Sociology professor named Dr. Mazarelli, who was very inspiring and supportive. I took a sociology introduction course with her. While I was in her class and office, Dr. Mazarelli acknowledged my efforts as a student. I could barely speak English then, but I was expected to express my thoughts on sociological issues, including cultural differences among ethnic groups that we discussed in class, in that new language. Through numerous conversations, Dr. Mazarelli inspired me to continue to study. She thought that I would make a good sociologist, which I never became at her disappointment.

After I finished my associate degree at Massachusetts Bay Community College, I transferred to University of Massachusetts-Boston to complete my bachelor's degree in social work with a minor in human advocacy, as my goal was to go to law school. However, I chose not to pursue such a goal, as I felt that not being a native English speaker would hinder me from successfully and effectively arguing and defending court cases. Later I realized that I was ill-thinking of myself, as there are many lawyers whose English is not their first language and they have been successful.

While working on my bachelor's, I took a class called *Moral Dilemma* with a professor named Ann Withorn, who, like Dr. Mazarelli, helped me believe in myself as an immigrant student. She was extremely supportive to me throughout my undergraduate studies at University of Massachusetts in Boston. She said that I was a good analyst and critical thinker. She, therefore, thought that I would be a good social policy analyst or a good lawyer. One day, she invited to come to her office to chat. While we were talking, she looked at me and asked: "Pierre, have you read the work of a well known Brazilian educator named Paulo Freire?" I responded saying "No." She proceeded to say: "You need to read one of his books; he just passed away."

That was in early fall 1997, and Paulo Freire had just died. Professor Withorn lent me a copy of one of Paulo Freire's books, *Pedagogy of the Oppressed*, and this book has changed my life as an educator. After she handed the book to me, she said with confidence, "You'll like it." I thanked her and left her office. I went home the same day and started reading this book. After I finished my bachelor's degree and went to complete my master's degree, Professor Withorn persuaded me to pursue a doctorate degree in social policy. I applied for it at

PREFACE   XV

Brandeis University located in Waltham, Massachusetts, and was denied acceptance despite receiving a strong letter of recommendation from her.

At the same university, I had the honor to study with a prominent sociolinguist and public intellectual, Dr. Donaldo Macedo, while I was working on my master's degree in Applied Linguistics. Professor Donaldo Macedo helped me better understand Freire's scholarly and political work. He was Paulo's close mentee and friend. He co-authored several books with Freire and translated many of his books. While I was a student there, Professor Macedo introduced us in class to fine African intellectuals like Frantz Fanon and Albert Memmi. Though I was already familiar with their work since high school, it was a breath of fresh air to revisit them in a much more critical way in Professor Macedo's class.

The two years I spent taking classes with Professors, like Donaldo Macedo and Pepi Leistyna, intellectually marked me. These two professors in particular challenged me to critically reflect on and analyze linguistic, racial, socio-economic, and political realities that affected (and continue to affect) my life and that of others. Other intellectuals and critical thinkers whom they talked about in class, such as Noam Chomsky, Sonia Nieto, Antonia Darder, Peter McLaren, Peter Mayo, Christine Sleeter, Cornel West, Henry Giroux, Joe Kincheloe, and Shirley Steinberg, among many others, have intellectually inspired me. Many of them would later become good colleagues and friends.

Some of them have supported me in many ways. For example, I often turn to some of them for advice when I need to make a major professional decision. Furthermore, while some have genuinely and graciously written forewords supporting my books, others have happily written letters of recommendation on my behalf. Still others, including Joe Kincheloe, have published some of my books in their book series while inspiring me to appreciate much more and understand better Paulo Freire's work by reading their work on\about Paulo Freire.

Freire's scholarly and activist work has helped me understand oppressive teaching practices that have been normalized in the school system, the unequal power relation between the powerful and those that have been forced in subordinate positions in society. Discovering *Pedagogy of the Oppressed* could not have been at a better more timely, for two years or so after I read it, I started teaching at a high school located in the most marginalized neighborhood in Boston, Massachusetts. As a novice teacher at this impoverished high school, I learned valuable teaching and life lessons that contributed to my becoming later a compassionate and committed social justice educator.

Specifically, I learned first-hand that, contrary to America's basic promises of equity, fairness, and equal access to quality education, bilingual immigrant students routinely experienced xenophobia, linguistic discrimination, and racial segregation in schools, in addition to facing socio-economic inequalities. I also learned from their stories about human resilience and a deep sense of hope for a better future. I begin this book with gratitude, as I strongly feel that it is important to do so. Without the influence of scholars and authors noted above, my academic and professional successes would not have been a reality.

Acknowledgements

I feel indebted to Professors Peter Mayo, Peter McLaren, Zeus Leonardo, and David Stovall, respectively, for having faith in this book by supporting it with heir amazing forewords, afterword, and blurbs. I am sincerely grateful for their support. Besides these genuine and prominent colleagues who have inspired and supported me in many ways, I am deeply grateful to my life mentor, my mother, who has been the most influential person in my life. Her life stories as a single mother raising several children have inspired me to face and overcome challenges that at times seem impossible. Specifically, when I am faced with personal and professional challenges, I make an effort to remember what my mother went through both as a teenager and later as a single mother.

Besides my mother, my spouse, children, brother, sister, nieces, nephews, cousins, dear friends, and some in laws have played a fundamental role in my human development, maturity, and prosperity. I am indebted to them. In addition to family and friends, former teachers, professors, and mentors have supported and inspired me to be where I am now. Specifically, while I was in high school, I had a history teacher named Jean Reynold Jean-Pierre, and the head of a youth center, Paul Ascencio (Polo), who were like mentors to me and other marginalized youth. These two individuals deeply inspired me.

I was fortunate to reconnect with Paul in 2015 along with my family after we had not seen each other for more than 20 years but seeing him felt as if it we had always been together. We reflected and talked about the past we shared as mentor and mentee. He drove us around his town and city of origin, Cape Haitian, to see historical sites that I learned about in history textbooks but did not have the opportunity to visit while I was residing in the island. It is one of the most memorable moments in my personal life and that of my family. Paul is an awesome guy! He and the history teacher inspired me to believe in myself. Thanks to their inspiration, I was able to enter into my inner self to find strength to combat abject poverty and transcend the shame of being a working class boy from the countryside. Their life stories, intellectual rigor, and words of encouragement inspired me to go beyond restricted academic borders to explore various forms of literature so that I could become a knowledgeable and well-informed world citizen.

Through their mentorship and teaching, I was introduced to authors and scholars, such as Eduardo Gaelano, Frantz Fanon, Gabriel Garcia Marquez, Jean Ziegler, Antenor Firmin, Jean Price Mars, Albert Memmi, Amical Cabral, Antonio Gramsci, Jacques Stephen Alexis, C.L.R. James, and Jacques Roumain whose work I read with avidity while I was in high school. Admittedly, out of all these writers and intellectuals, the scholarly and activist work of Frantz Fanon has influenced my intellectual landscape at the deepest level. Reading Fanon has enabled me to gain a sound understanding of the awful effects of racism and colonialism on colonized people and the cultural, psychological, and material conditions of people of African descent in general. Frantz Fanon is my intellectual hero par excellence. The support, influence, and inspiration of the people noted above have helped me with the intellectual and academic preparation needed to write this book. However, the person who has inspired me the most and has planted the fire in me to write this book is my mother, who just turned 85 years old; she has given me the human oxygen to sustain myself throughout my personal, academic, and professional journey. My mother is incomparable.

Introduction

Stories matter. They reflect one's journey, from which other people can learn life lessons. It is important for people, particularly historically marginalized ones, to share their stories so that they can be preserved, and, most importantly, so that the younger generation can learn from them. Many people have done so through podcast interviews, songs, art, poetry, narratives, and auto-ethnography.

This auto-ethnographic book draws from personal, academic, and professional experiences to document my ontological journey as a Black man growing up in the Ghetto and currently laboring in the Ivy halls of the United States of America – a country where people of color, including professionals, like myself, have been racially discriminated targeted. Paradoxically, it is the same America where I have been academically and professionally successful. I have attributed my attainments to access to opportunities and resources as well as mentorship and support from family members, friends, colleagues, and former professors. However, besides fortunate historical accidents that led to my academic and professional accomplishments, this book captures my complex existential experiences shaped by the violence of poverty, sexual harassment that I experienced with a sexual predator, political turmoil and corruption that I endured in my birth land, as well as the vicious cycle of systemic racism, White supremacy, and xenophobia that I would later be facing in America.

Before deciding to write this book, however, I asked myself questions, such as: Why write it at this present time? Should I wait? After critically examining the thoughts and feelings that prompted these questions, I asked myself this question: Why not now? Admittedly, at first, though not the primary reason, fearing that I might die young, like may Black and Brown men, led me to hurry to write this book. I then realized that I had to transcend this fear, and I had.

The best possible way in which I can interpret such fear is that I have already known too many young men of color who have been murdered or who have died of massive heart attacks as a result of racial fatigue and trauma. Their death has made me think seriously about my own life as a Black man. Systemic racism, manifested in the form of racial profiling, micro-aggression, denial of employment or job promotion, and lack of access to quality education and health care, has caused Black people develop illnesses, like high blood pressure, diabetes, and heart disease, leading to their early death (Kozol, 2011). The root causes of heart attacks that have taken the lives of many people of color might be hard for racially privileged groups to understand, especially those

© KONINKLIJKE BRILL NV, LEIDEN, 2020 | DOI: 10.1163/9789004440944_001

who do not have much awareness about institutional racism. However, for people of color, myself included, this is not hard at all to comprehend.

As a case in point, I knew fairly well a Black lawyer and a community organizer who worked with young Black and Latino men and women in a marginalized city in western Massachusetts. He died of a massive heart attack while he was only 41 year old. Close friends and relatives were shocked about his sudden death, for there is no one in his family who had died of a heart attack. Some people speculated the massive heart attack that took his life might have been caused by racial fatigue rooted in institutional racism he experienced. Such a speculation makes sense to me as a Black man who has been experiencing both racial fatigue and micro aggression too frequently. These forms of oppression have affected the health of many Black people, young and old, and I am not an exception.

Research shows that the life expectancy of Black people living in the United States is shorter than their White counterparts (Bonilla-Silva, 2003/2018). Racism is a pandemic and it has adversely affected the life of people of color in various ways-psychologically, racially, educationally, socio-economically, and politically. In my native land, Haiti, I personally experienced classism, colorism, and sexism, but not racism as a Black man until I moved to the United States. In Haiti, poverty was so rampant in my social milieu that I breathed it almost every day. For example, I witnessed abject poverty in the underfunded, dilapidated and collapsing schools that I attended as well as the poor neighborhoods where I grew up and hang out with my friends and siblings.

By visiting close friends and classmates living in marginalized places, such as Cite Soleil, known as the "ghost" city in Haiti, and comparing these places to the relatively clean and safe neighborhoods where the rich lived, I was able to have a clear sense of classism. Also, by attending a poorly funded public high school, *Lycee Petion*, located next to a well-resourced catholic high school, *Petit Seminaire College St. Martial*, it was not hard for me to distinguish poor Haitian students from the privileged ones. While the rich students wore nice clothes and shoes to go to school, and were often dropped off and picked up by parents in fancy cars, the poor students often wore second hand clothes and had to walk miles to and from school. I was one of these students, so were many of my close friends and classmates. Finally, knowing neighbors, friends, and extended family members who could not feed themselves and send their children to school helped me understand abject poverty.

In addition to poverty, this book captures other forms of systemic oppression, including racism, White supremacy and xenophobia, which I have faced in the United States. This book seeks to shed light on these issues from perspectives holistically rooted in my lived experiences as a Black man first

INTRODUCTION   3

and foremost as well as a Black university professor laboring in predominantly White institutions in the powerful country on earth, the United States.
The world powerful, however, needs to be critically analyzed and decon-
structed here, for it often entails the domination and conquest of vulnerable
countries by more powerful countries.

1   Overview of the Book

In the first three chapters,[1] I begin by talking about my upbringings, including
ignoring my unearned male and heterosexual privileges as a straight Black
man growing up in a very sexist and homophobic country in the Caribbean,
Haiti. I choose to do so as I feel that it is important to examine unearned privileges that I have benefited from the patriarchal system. In addition to my male
and heterosexual privileges, I have class privileges as a university professor.
It is important that I acknowledge the privileges that I have been fortunate to
have, despite my daily struggles with institutional racism, White supremacy
and xenophobia.

In these chapters, I specifically talk about my experiences as a working
class man growing up in the poorest country economically in the western
hemisphere yet culturally and historically rich, I go on to explicate the socio-
economic and political circumstances that led to my migration to the United
States and the manner in which I have been experiencing systemic racism,
White supremacy, and xenophobia as well as how I have courageously faced
these systemic forms of oppression. I go on to explain how my view about
race has changed ever since. I situate my blackness in the context of the
United States, where my daily experience with racism has reminded me that
I am Black.

Substantiating further the points that I made in the previous chapters, in
the subsequent chapters, I articulate many forms of systemic oppression to
which I have experienced (and continue to experience) and witnessed other
people of color being subjected in the United States. In the last two chapters,
I describe in depth my experience with systemic racism as a Black professor
teaching and doing research in predominantly White colleges and universities. In these institutions, sometimes I feel invisible, while other times I feel
visible, particularly when it serves the interests of the university stakehold-
ers. I describe multiple forms of systemic oppression, including micro aggression, which I have experienced both as a Black student and professor. I argue
that despite years of beautiful struggles before becoming a university professor, despite my current status and class privileges, I am not and will not be

protected from institutional racism and White supremacy. To simply put it, my social class status can change, and it has indeed changed. However, I can't ever change the fact that I am Black, and people have discriminated against me because of my blackness.

2 Conclusion

This book reflects my personal, academic, and professional journey both in the developing and developed world, Haiti and the United States, respectively. While racism and xenophobia have been savage forms of systemic oppression I have been fighting against in the United States, I faced classism and accentism (i.e. discrimination based on one's accent, often associated with one's country of origin, social class, and native tongue, etc.). Our experiences as Black people are not homogenous, for our ethnicity, culture, nationality, social class, religion, gender, and sexuality have shaped us differently besides race. There are differences in immigrant status, gender, social class, sex, language, [dis]ability, and age that make all of us unique as human beings. For example, the daily reality of an African American might not be the same as a poor Black immigrant. Likewise, the lived experiences of an able-bodied Black person is not the same as that of a physically, emotionally, and psychologically limited person of color. Finally, the daily challenges of a gay, bisexual, or transgender Black person is not same as a heterosexual and middle class Black person. While the former might be primarily concerned about racism, the latter has to deal with this systemic oppression and homophobia. This is simply to say that my stories, although might reflect the reality of other men of color, should not be used to generalize about their lives.

Note

1 Major parts of Chapters 1, 3 and 4 were previously published in my first book *Education under Occupation* but are significantly revised here for the purpose of this book.

CHAPTER 1

Home and Early Literacy Memories

Giving an account thus takes a narrative form, which not only depends on the ability to relay a set of sequential events with plausible transitions but also draws upon narrative voice and authority, being directed toward an audience with the aim of persuasion. The narrative must then establish that the self either was or was not the cause of that suffering, and so supply a persuasive medium through which to understand the causal agency of the self. The narrative does not emerge after the fact of causal agency but constitutes the prerequisite condition for any account of moral agency we might give. In this sense, narrative capacity constitutes a precondition for giving an account of oneself and assuming responsibility for one's actions through that means.

> JUDITH BUTLER, *Giving an Account of Oneself* (2005, p. 12)

∙∙
∙

I begin this book with an autobiographical account where I recollect both my childhood and adolescent memories from my birth land. I recollect such memories through a thick description of various life events that occurred during the epoch I lived there. To me, giving an account of one's self requires one to "go back to the source," as Cabral (1973) puts it, in order to reconstruct memories, including social memory. It is important to do so particularly because, as Bell (2010) notes, "As a bridge between past and present, social memory shapes identity, informs our interpretations of events, fuels grievances and claims on the present, and suggests what we might imagine for the future" (p. 47). What follows is a detailed account of my lived experiences being born to a rural working-class family in Haiti.

1 Recollect My Childhood and Adolescence Memories

I was born in Port-au-Prince, the capital of Haiti. However, from birth until I was 11 years old or so, I lived in a small rural place called Beauge, located about 60 miles from Port-au-Prince and 300 miles from the Dominican Republic. I am

© KONINKLIJKE BRILL NV, LEIDEN, 2020 | DOI: 10.1163/9789004440944_002

the youngest of my mothers' seven children and one out of the four that have survived. My older siblings and I were born out of wedlock. My father was, too, born out of wedlock. He was already married and had with 7 children with his wife when he met my mother, who had recently gotten out of an oppressive relationship with her former husband with whom she had twin daughters. One of my twin sisters died while she was only 3 months old, while the other who survived became mentally ill in her adult life for several years and was never fully recovered until she died while she was only 43 years old. Similar to my mother, my eldest sister gave birth to 6 children and only two of them have survived.

I felt sheltered and over protected growing up. My older siblings treated me as if I was their own child, even though there was not a huge age gap between us. In Haiti, it is culturally expected of older siblings to take care of the younger ones. I felt loved and supported as a child, for I had families, neighbors, and my parents' friends who cared for me and continue to do so to this day. My father was a carpenter, who did not know how to read or write, while my mother was an entrepreneur, who did not go beyond sixth grade. When my mother was about 14-year old, she was forced to drop out of school to work with her mother, who was aging. Though she was the youngest child alive in the family, my mother was proven to be the most reliable one through her behavior and action. My deceased uncle, who was older than her, was not trusted to be dependable. Therefore, my grandmother counted on my mother, who later became the main breadwinner of the family.

As a single parent, my mother toiled in the most extreme conditions to support her children and her aging mother. She often had to leave us behind with her mother for days to go to a remote area in Haiti called Fond Verrettes to sell alimentary products, like rice, beans, and sugar, to street vendors who, in turn, resold what they bought from her in order to be able to provide for themselves and their families. In Haiti, this type of informal commercial transaction is happening everywhere and has been the means by which working class people have survived, particularly the masses. My most humble experience with my mother was when she took my siblings and I to visit her in Fond Verrettes where she did most her commercial transactions as an entrepreneur.

Fonds Verrettes was, and still is, cold. It's located near the Dominican Republic – a country that shares a border with Haiti. While visiting my mother, I was saddened to see the tiny and cold room where she was sleeping. This room was nothing but a beat-up little storage made of dirt floor and leaky roof, with no electricity. My mother used a lamp at night to read her Holy bible and also to get around her tiny room. Although I was happy to visit the place where my mother was earning a living to raise us, I was shocked by the conditions she was living in. I immediately wanted to go back to Beauge where I was living. At the same time, witnessing the condition in which my mother labored to provide for us inspired me to develop much respect, admiration, and love for her in particular and working class single mothers in general. My mother toiled in such condition for nearly forty years until her body gave up on her. After my mother reached her late 50s, she was no longer physically able to do this type of job, which required much more physical strength than she had left.

Fortunately, around the same time when my mother stopped laboring, my older brother managed to immigrate to the United States to seek a better life. He immediately became the main provider of the whole family since my mother could no longer work and my father deserted us soon after my brother left the country. They and my older siblings sacrificed their lives, including their education, to support me throughout my schooling and beyond, and I am infinitely indebted to them for their sacrifice and unconditional love.

2 Early Literacy

When I was a child, I used to hear my mother saying to people, including people she met on the street, who inquired about me, "Oh, he is the last drop. I almost did not have him." My mother would say this aloud with a smile on her face. She expressed herself freely like the typical working class women in her community usually did. I often wondered why my mother was so loud and why she would describe me that way. Was it because she felt embarrassed for having me when she was in her mid 30s? Working class women at the time usually had, and still have, children much younger than the middle class ones? Was it because I was very frail as a child? I wondered. In my neighborhood, walking with a child who looked frail was an embarrassment for working class parents. Did my mother feel ashamed of me because of my physical appearance? I pondered.

My mother also made similar comments to people who showed curiosity about me during Sunday church. Every Sunday, my mother would take me to church with her. I had no idea as to why I needed to be there, but my mother insisted that I went to church with her every Sunday. She also made sure my cloths were well ironed for this special day: Sunday church. Whether I wanted to skip church, I could not. I had no choice but accompanied her; she was, and still is, a matriarch. It was not until I moved to the city that I was able to make my own decision about the Sunday church, which I eventually stopped attending. Years later, I would go back to church of my liking and when I felt the need to go but not through coercion.

Growing up, my mother's bible was the only book that I had access to at home besides the textbooks of my older siblings. These textbooks were always in my siblings' backpacks, which were not within my reach. I did not grow up listening to bedtime stories that middle class parents usually told their children. However, my mother always read her bible aloud at night, and I was always close to her. As my mother's youngest child, I was told that I often fell asleep in her arms as she was reading her Bible. She, at times, burst into tears, full of emotions, as she was reading certain verses in the bible. I never could comprehend why she got very emotional when she was reading the bible. She also cried every time she was singing the *Amazing Grace* song, and I never knew why, for she never explained. Nonetheless, this was her ritual every night before she went to bed and in the morning after she woke up. I bore witness to, and was part of this ritual, until I immigrated to the United States in my early 20s. When I go back home annually to visit my mother, I get to experience the same ritual but differently: I can now understand everything she says, whereas as a child I could not.

My mother was nearly 60 years old when she stopped working, as she got older and was thus unable to take care of heavy sacks of rice, beans, sugar, and salt that she sold in bulks to local street vendors who, in turn, resold them in smaller quantity to local buyers, in order to earn an honest living. As noted earlier, this commercial transaction was a form of economy of auto-substantiality practiced by local Haitian farmers among themselves. This form of transaction is still occurring around the country, although it has been impacted by massive flows of imported alimentary products from abroad, particularly the United States. That is, local famers and merchants have gone bankrupt as the price of locally grown food has gone up and that of imported products, usually of lower quality, has gone down.

Consumers, particularly working class people, were, and still are, gravitated toward imported products, as they tended to be cheaper than the local ones. This led to the financial crisis that local farmers, who depended, and still depend, on selling locally grown crops at local markets to sustain themselves and their families, had frequently experienced and continue to experience. Because my mother could not continue doing this physically challenging job, she retired. However, she never received any compensation from the government, even though she paid taxes all her life. After my mother retired, my older brother, who had recently managed to immigrate to the United States, immediately took over the family's financial responsibility. We did not receive much support from my father, who at that point was financially struggling with several children with his wife and another mistress other than my mother.

3   Attending School in the Countryside

I formally started going to school when I was about 5 years old. My mother decided to keep me at home because, according to the cultural norms and beliefs held by working class parents in the countryside, which she believed in, I was too young to even start kindergarten. Some parents even kept their children until they felt they were six before they started to formally go to school. Working class parents at the time felt that way, whereas those who were middle-class felt and acted differently; the latter often moved to the capital, Port-au Prince, or a nearby larger city so that their children could go to a "good" school and on time. By good school, it is meant those that were well-resourced, including having well-prepared and better paid teachers. Many of my friends and neighbors that I grew up with in Beauge started school late and finished, for example, high school in their early or mid 20s. Like many of them, I completed high school at the age of 22.

I attended and received my basic education in a Christian school built in Beauge by White American evangelical missionaries. This school, which still stands but looks beaten from outside, was used simultaneously as a preschool, elementary, and middle school attended by poor working class children residing in Beauge. The school, which was made of bricks, was literally attached to the backyard of a church sponsored by the same White American missionaries. The office of the school principal, along with the classrooms and the kitchen, were placed behind the church. The playground where I often played soccer with my working classmates during recess was located on the left side of the church facing some shanty houses where many working class farmers lived. Some of these farmers' children attended that school.

Poor working class women from the neighborhood where the school was located were hired to prepare free breakfast and free lunch for students. These women worked long hours and were paid very little; they never complained publically against their exploitative conditions; they did not have other employment options that were more lucrative than the meager salary they were receiving from White American evangelical missionaries. Teachers, too, received meager salary, and they were silent about it, as employment, like teaching in the countryside, was scare – there was only school in Beauge and surrounding areas at the time. From what I recall, classrooms were crowded, and teachers did not have adequate resources to effectively teach school children. However, as I am reminded, most of them showed that they cared for us; at times, with their meager salary, some of the teachers, especially those who moved from the city to teach in the countryside, helped students in need in the community where I lived.

I had access to early literacy from this Christian school-church that the White American missionaries built. Specifically, my parents could only afford to send me to receive basic reading, writing, and math skills and civic lessons at that school, where I was also introduced to Christianity. As a young boy, I learned about the bible, not in a critical way, to which the school principal, besides my mother, introduced me. Those who disobeyed the school principal, named Yvonne, were punished. I often got frustrated with her insisting that we went to church even tough many of my friends did not want to do so. I resented her for that until I left the school. I also resented my mother who pressured me to do the same thing. Nonetheless, despite this oppressive religious practice and the lack of adequate resources that both teachers and students experienced at the school, it was there I learned my ABC and started the learning process of socialization.

I, at times, skipped school to experience learning beyond the classroom wall through self-discovery in the woods, where I hunted birds as an alternative for meat, which was at times scare at home. Somehow I never got caught skipping classes, and I wondered how many students who might have done the same thing and got away with it. Ironically, this was the school where one of my teachers, Mrs. Marie, told me that I was very smart and that I would go far in life if I applied myself. She witnessed that I played and talked a lot in class. She, at times, hit me with a ruler out of frustration when I was not paying attention to her while she was talking. That same teacher forced me to use my right hand to write instead of my left hand as soon as she realized that I was left-handed.

Her action psychologically affected me to this day; yet, she was THE teacher who kept saying to me that I was too smart to be playing with peers who did not take their studies seriously and that she would talk to my parents about it if I did not stop fooling around. Even though I rebelled in her class, she did not give up on me. Internally, I was hungry to learn but I was disturbed by the violence and trauma of poverty, which I did not know how to name then. I used school, including her classroom, to release my anger about it, but such anger was taken for something else because of the way I expressed it, as I realized decades later. Mrs. Marie was kind and patient with me in my learning process, even though her teaching method was too traditional. She often had us repeat after her, including songs, which I found annoying. I eventually lost interest in her teaching method and style but was still hunger to learn. I eventually failed her class, which I had to repeat.

As I became a teenager, I found my intellectual and academic refuge in books, and that was when my learning curve began. Books became the daily bread that I felt that I needed to have to complement for my mis-education. Through reading, I interrogated and unlearned many things that I learned

HOME AND EARLY LITERACY MEMORIES

about gender roles and cultural norms; as I elaborated later, some of these roles and norms were oppressive. Through avid reading, I became more knowledgeable about my history and culture. I abhorred school but I loved learning through natural and self-discovery with books. At school, I was always told that I was either too quiet or too hyper. Depending on the teacher, I was labeled as either too talkative or too quiet. I often questioned things that seemed normal and thus acceptable to my peers, like class and gender inequities.

My father enrolled me in a poorly funded middle school that one of his friends – a deceased Haitian reverend – was in charge of. That school was located in a different town about three miles away from where I lived. I used my older brother's bike to get there. People living nearby the school were, and still are, poor working class farmers. As I recall, the road leading to that school was in terrible shape. I had to fix the bike quite often, as it was affected by sharp stones and rocks spread on the road while riding back to and from school.

However, riding the bike helped me avoid old childhood friends on the street who would have asked me why I moved back to the countryside from Port-au-Prince, if they had the opportunity to ask. I imagine they would have wanted to know why I returned to Beauge because rarely did people move back to the countryside after having moved to the city. In people's eyes, doing so was a set back, which was indeed the case. My single mother could no longer continue to afford the cost of living in the city, namely Port-au-Prince. Therefore, I, along with my siblings, had to return to the countryside where we had a house and family members. I was disappointed because I was already used to the city life. When I first returned, I had to hide from my childhood friends and former classmates, as I felt ashamed. I was afraid that they would make fun of me, as returning back home to the countryside was unusual. People who left the countryside for the city rarely returned home, although after the earthquake in 2010 many Haitians were forced to go back to where they were from, as Port-au-Prince was nearly destroyed. Otherwise, this usually happens when people are financially bankrupt. I sensed that my neighbors and friends knew that I was forced to come back to the countryside.

The principal of the middle school that I attended decided to skip me 1 grade, specifically sixth grade, as he felt that I was ready to be placed in seventh grade. However, I felt that his decision, which my father approved, impacted me academically, with respect to mathematics particularly. I felt pressured to prove myself constantly while I was struggling with mathematics. I was often confused about math, which I still find challenging. I remember having math anxiety each time my math teacher would enter the classroom. Throughout middle school, I struggled learning math adequately but was determined to improve it in high school, and I somewhat did. I had to do so that I could pass a competitive college admission test containing a math section. I was never provided with the support that I needed to excel in math as a student but somehow managed, on my own, to improve such an important skill.

I suppose the school principal and the main teacher recommended that I skipped sixth grade based on my previous grades, which were very good. It was not my father's fault that I struggled a bit in both seventh and eighth grades – he was just a carpenter who was following teachers' advice; teachers were the experts in my parents' mind. Hence, whatever they said was the gospel truth. I was abruptly placed in the middle of the academic year in a totally different school environment with totally different classmates and teachers. To make matter worse, I was also placed in a higher grade than I was fully prepared for – mathematics was my demon and I needed extra help to fight it but I did not receive it.

Although I did very well at that school earning the third highest regional score on the official state standardized test that students had to take before starting high school, I still did not have confidence in math. But I was determined to earn it. One of my deceased cousins knew that math was my biggest challenge; so he often offered to swing by the window where my math classroom was located to drop answers about math problems that I was asked to solve during final examinations. However, I did not accept such offer from him. Instead, I decided to work on my math skill reaching out to classmates and friends for help along the way. I never hesitated to ask for help when I needed to do so, and this has been part of my philosophy, at leastacademically.

When I was not in school, I played soccer with friends, usually barefooted. This was normal practice for us as working class kids. We played hide and seek at night during full moon. I experienced *no fear of the other* that now haunts many inhabitants residing in the beautiful country that I left over two decades ago. Even though I experienced abject poverty growing up, I was happy and had the best childhood experiences. I felt safe and loved. I had access to organic food and hand-made clothing, which local tailors made. While living there, I felt closer to nature and safe from environmental chemicals, and from strangers in the street. There was a sense of belonging, which I still cherish.

At home, we did not have any books except my mother's bible and textbooks of my older siblings. From the Holy Bible, my mother read verses aloud before we all went to bed. Reading her bible aloud was in a way my bedtime story and early literacy exposure. Still, to this day, my mother holds on her bible, which she reads throughout the day and night. The Holy Scripture has become her most loyal and consistent companion. She is now in her 80s, and she does not go anywhere without holding her bible tight in her right hand.

While living in Beauge, I had no access to running water, electricity, telephone, or television. At night, I used lamps as primary light to read and do my homework. My family did not own a car, a TV or expensive furniture. My mother owned a very modest house where my siblings and I lived. Unfortunately, the foundation of that house degenerated over time. The floor was worn to dirt in some places, while parts of the ceiling leaked. My single mother could not repair the house, as her income could only afford her to feed us and send us to school.

My father helped whenever he could or wanted. He sometimes punished my mother (us) when he was upset with her by discontinuing to provide financial assistance. Witnessing my single mother raising four of us in a tiny house located in a poor and underdeveloped rural area with no access to electricity or clean water and almost no support from my father helped me develop critical awareness and consciousness about class and gender inequities and their harmful effects on women, particularly hard working class. Female street venders in my neighborhood worked hard only to barely feed their families. Yet, their husbands often beat them up for no apparent reason.

My mother and father were separated when I was about 15 years old. Even before my parents were separated, I barely saw my father in the house; he came home only when mother was there. As I noted earlier, my mother spent most of her time outside the house selling alimentary products in Fonds Verrette. As a child, I was left with and taken care by my older siblings, a nannie, my mother's cousins, and neighbors who all played the role of my parents. Whenever I needed to see my father, I had to go to his carpentry shop, which was about two miles away from where my mother's modest house was located.

Growing up, I lived part of my adolescent and teenage years through difficult times. There was a time when my mother could not feed us. She was forced to ask nearby neighbors to sell her basic food, such as rice, beans, sweet potatoes, and corn, so that we would not be starved. The most shameful experience I ever had was when these neighbors came to my house asking my mother to pay them back and she did have the money to do so. Like my mother and my other older siblings, I felt deeply ashamed and burst into tears. Some of these neighbors often threatened my mother that they would not sell her any alimentary product unless she had the money to pay them back.

I felt deeply hurt in my heart, when I witnessed some of these neighbors raising their voice on my mother, who helplessly put one of her arms behind her neck perhaps out of embarrassment and shame, and she looked defeated. Tears came out of my mothers' eyes as soon as the neighbors left. The saddest part of all this was that some of these neighbors were people my mother used to support a lot financially by lending them money and buying them food before they managed to own their small grocery stores. This factor alone was devastating to my mother who later called them in her mother tongue "ingra" (i.e., people without gratitude). This experience and countless others created the deepest psychological mark in my memory and soul and consequently helped me develop consciousness about class and gender inequalities, particularly in a rural context.

Although my family had gone through financial hardships growing up, I felt that we were culturally, spiritually, and communally rich. There was a sense of community, and I felt safe therein. Many of my neighbors were like my extended family. They looked after me when my mother was not around. My family's problems were my neighbors' and vice versa. Although Beauge is located in an underdeveloped rural area, I enjoyed living there. I felt close to nature and learned to appreciate the natural beauty of life in the countryside. I was not exposed to chemical waste. Nor did I smell unhealthy odors from piled-up trashes as I did later when I moved to Port-au-Prince. While living in Beauge, neither children nor adults dig into big piles of discarded waste looking for food, secondhand shoes, and other basic necessities, as was the case in the shantytowns where I lived in the capital of Haiti. However, I witnessed men unfairly treating women who were (and still are) the spines of the Haitian society.

4 Gender Inequities

In Beauge, where my mother still lives, most men and women were farmers during the time when I was living there. Men usually worked all day in the farm, sometimes with their wives and their children, especially when school was not in session. Even though these female farmers spent all day working with their husband in the farm, they still had to cook, clean the house, wash and iron their husbands' and children's clothes when they returned home. The few men and women who were not primarily farmers were entrepreneurs, street vendors, taxi drivers, small truck drivers, and carpenters. My parents fit in some of these categories.

Although my father was trained as a carpenter, he did some farming on the side; he hired people to cultivate lands that he both owned and of which he was in charge. Similarly, even though my mother was an entrepreneur who sold goods, she also did some farming on the side. She, too, hired people to grow corn, beans, and sweet potatoes on the lands her parents left her behind, of which she has greatly benefited to this day. She additionally paid people to take care of her animals, like cows, goats, chicken, and pigs. Like many of

HOME AND EARLY LITERACY MEMORIES

her female cousins and other women in the neighborhood, my mother was expected by my father to assume domestic tasks, like cooking, cleaning, and washing our clothes, including my fathers' underwear when she returned home from work. It did not matter how tired my mother was; she was expected to fulfill domestic tasks.

Like many boys in my community, I first learned how to "be a man" from my parents, particularly my father. "Being a man" in my parents' view, especially in that of my father's, was to have as many girls as I wanted, to not show any emotion or sign of weakness, but instead to be in charge of the house when he was not around even though my sisters were older than I was. The misconception about "being a man" also reflected and translated into the way the domestic tasks were divided in my house. My mother always made sure that she or my sisters ironed my clothes, my brother's, as well as my father's. She also cooked and cleaned the house. My job was to focus on my studies. At no time do I remember my mother asking me, or my brother, to help her with any type of chore in the house. Even though my sisters were in school and had do to their homework, they were expected to take care of all domestic tasks, while my brother and I were able to concentrate on our studies and later play outdoors with our male friends if we wanted to.

I could spend almost the whole day outside the house playing dominoes and soccer, hunting birds or fishing with my male friends without having to worry about any chore that needed to be taken care of in the house or meals that needed to be prepared. I had fun playing with my male friends with no worries, for I knew my sisters would take care of the cleaning, the cooking, the washing, and the ironing of our clothes. They, however, were not allowed to spend too much time outside the house because (1) they needed to be home to take care of the house and (2) my parents were afraid that they would be playing with boys and get pregnant. My sisters' freedom was often taken away from them because of socially constructed sexual and gender roles, while mine was given to me without having to fight for it.

My sisters were not the only ones who were deprived of the freedom that my brother, other boys, and I enjoyed in my neighborhood. There were other girls and women who were also oppressed by their own mothers and fathers, who tried to control every angle of their lives. Like my sisters, their gender, sex, and body were under surveillance. By surveillance, I mean a set of established rigid cultural codes and practices that infringe the freedom of historically oppressed groups and lead to their oppression.

At a young age, the difference between boys and girls was already inculcated in my mind. I was not allowed to play with dolls, but playing with fake guns, helicopters, and cars was encouraged. When I became a teenager, this difference became clearer to me. I was expected to fight and be good at it, although I never did so. I was also expected to play sports, such as soccer, which I did, and still do. I was expected to have more 1 girlfriend, and I acted on that expectation. I was praised for it by my male friends, my brother, father, and even by some of my female siblings. However, my sisters could not do the same. Had they dared do so, they would have been called names, like bitches and pervert, ridiculed, and severely punished by my parents. Some of the common punishments entailed taking young girls out of school, which was harsh, or sending them somewhere else to live temporarily with another relative, who was expected to straighten them out before they were sent back to their parents.

In fact, something similar happened to one of my sisters, who was "dating" the principal of her school. This principal, who was about 14 years older than my sister, who was at that time 15 years old, covertly "dated" my sister for about a year until my father found out about it. As soon as he did, he stopped paying for the education of my sister, who was forced to stay out of school for about a year. Instead of filing a complaint about the school principal, who abused his male power, my father blamed my sister who was actually a victim.

Distorted view of maleness was the norm, and this negatively impacted the daily life of girls, women, and, to a great extent, that of men in the community where I grew up. I am reminded of how good my male friends made me feel when I told them that two of my girlfriends, who were neighbors, fought over me. I was only 16 years old. My father somehow learned about the fight and bragged to his employees about it, who in turn welcomed me with a great smile when I went to visit him at his shop.

My father had about ten people who worked for him, and they were all men. They often made sexist jokes about women living in my neighborhood. Most of these men were married and had some mistresses. Their daily gossip was mostly about women, whom many of them perceived as sexual objects. In their view, generally women were good for sex and taking care of men and children. I was exposed to this discourse on a regular basis. Even though I was a kid, they felt quite comfortable talking in front of me in derogatory terms about women, especially the poor ones.

They talked "nicely" about women who had a great body, which essentially equated to having a big ass, and they scorned those who did not. Women without a big ass did not fit the category of "beautiful" women. They also often talked about women who they assumed were easy to get in bed with and those who were not. Moreover, they gossiped about women who cheated on their husbands or boyfriends. They had a name for these women, "bouzin," which essentially means "bitch" in English. Both men and women in my neighborhood

HOME AND EARLY LITERACY MEMORIES

looked down on these "bouzin" even though most of the men were dying to sleep with them. For these men, sleeping with any of these "bouzin" was like having a piece of the pie, for in their eyes these women were just objects.

Some men had beaten girlfriends or wives with impunity, especially those who were unfaithful. This violent act became normalized in the community where I spent the first decade or so of my life. The most known case that I remember of was that of a truck driver's wife. That brave woman transgressed the social norm established in the community that expected women to be faithful to their partners, husbands, or boyfriends, who, in the meantime, could have as many mistresses as they desired. She was caught cheating on her husband, who beat her numerous times, but he was never punished for his brutal sexist action. There was not even a legal action taken against his violent action. After being physically and psychologically abused by her husband, this woman left Haiti for the Dominican Republic, where she lived for about a year. When she returned to Haiti, she ironically went back to her abusive husband who continued beating her until her family helped her leave this violent relationship.

That woman was my mother's distant cousin. Some women in my neighborhood accepted abuses from their men, others fought back by standing up to them. My mother was one of the brave women. She stood up to her ex-husband (not my father) who was abusive. That is, he wanted to have sexual intercourse with mother whom doctor recommended that she waited for about six months before she did so. Her husband did not believe her and wanted to have sexual intercourse with her, and she refused. He became very violent toward my mother, who had to leave the house in the middle of the night to seek support from family members nearby. My mother and her family forced him to leave Haiti for the Dominican Republic, after he tried to sexually assault my mother, who had just given birth to two female twins. I support my mother's action to stand up to her former husband, as I believe that no one has control over one's body. Therefore, no one should be physically assaulted. Unfortunately, because of systemic oppression, including patriarchy, senseless crime has been committed against women and other groups who happen to be different. In the case of women, many were sexually harassed and molested while at the same time facing poverty and other forms of oppression.

In my neighborhood, both men and women were sometimes passive spectators of the brutality against women. Depending on the circumstances and the reason that led a man to beat his wife or girlfriend, sometimes a male relative of that wife or girlfriend would intervene to protect her from being killed by her husband or boyfriend. Sometimes, as it was in the case of my mother's distant cousin, the family of a woman who got beaten for cheating on her husband would not do anything to protect her, as some people believed that was a normal thing for a man to severely punish a wife or a girlfriend who cheated on him.

Another wrong reason for the justification of their silence about the physical and psychological abuses of females is that many men often felt ashamed that their sister, daughter, or female cousin cheated on their husband or boy friend. In this community, men, through their behavior and action (or lack thereof) simply perpetuated and strengthened the patriarchal system. This system worked to their advantage in that they did not have to worry about being looked down upon, scorned, being rejected by the community, or worse yet beaten by their wives or girlfriends if they deliberately cheated on them.

While women who cheated on their partners were called names and horribly looked down upon in my community, male cheaters were praised and seen as "bon jenjan," that is, as men who knew how to sweet talk women to go out with them and eventually get them in bed. Ironically, their male friends, fathers, and mothers usually praised them. Moreover, these male cheaters were the ones who often got more attention from women. Many of these women wanted to be with such men for their popularity despite the fact that they knew they were cheaters. In most cases, the decision of these women to be with men who were abusive and cheaters was informed by socioeconomic inequities. That is, men with some economic capital exploited the misery of many poor women, both young and old, by financially seducing them with gifts and empty promises for sexual exploitation.

Some of my male cousins, fell into this category of men. In my neighborhood, most women, including my mother, knew that these men were married. Yet, they ended up being their mistresses. The poor choice of my mother and countless other women is linked to the oppression rooted in a patriarchal system in Haiti that afforded men more economic opportunities than women. The institutionalization of the patriarchal system was such in my community that it was quite normal for men to have a wife and one or more mistresses. This is still happening in my community and other communities in Haiti. It is worth emphasizing that my mother's horrible social, economic, and psychological conditions and those of many women were the end result of an unjust socioeconomic and political system. This system established a labor force that enabled men to have more job opportunities than women, although this would later change with the Western globalization.

With this form of globalization, many factories were implanted in the Caribbean, particularly in Haiti, Jamaica, and the Dominican Republic, where there was a great concentration of female workers. These workers worked long hours like modern slaves in these factories, selling their cheap labor to Disney and

Nike that maximized their profits. Other Haitian women were and continue to be oppressed in other ways. My mother, my older sister, and many of their female cousins were among them. For example, while my sister became an entrepreneur selling goods on the street, I was in college studying. My father supported me with my schooling while he did not support my sister with hers. Many men reproduced the sexist behavior of their father, older brothers, and male cousins. In short, I grew up bearing witness to and participating in gender inequity through my silence, as I detailed in the following chapter.

CHAPTER 2

Questioning My Black Male and Heterosexual Privileges

To retrace and fully recapture my journey as a teenager and then as a man, it is necessary to build on the recollection of my childhood and adolescence memories, including exposure to patriarchal, homophobic, and classist views learned in various communities where I lived and grew up in Haiti. According to Sigmund Freud (1995), childhood and adolescence memories fundamentally shape people's characteristics and personality. I concur with Freud's idea, for as I reflect on memories dating back to my childhood and adolescence, I am able to locate where and how I acquired some of the homophobic and sexist views that I held for years about the LBGTQ community and women. I had some homophobic views about gay men that I had to unlearn as a result of my traumatic experience with sexual harassment from a gay male predator. I unlearned these views, which I elaborate on later in this chapter, and I have been trying to use my unearned privileges a straight Black man to combat heterosexual normativity.

1 Teenage and Young Adult Life Remembrances

I was about 16 years old when one of my father's employees told me that there was a woman who came to complain to my father about me because I was dating her daughter. She complained to my dad about this relationship because she felt that it was interfering with her daughter's education and domestic shore. She claimed that because her daughter was going out with me she could not concentrate on her studies. She also told my father that I was responsible for her daughter's inconsistency in cleaning the house, cooking, and washing clothes for her siblings. She summarized her complaint by saying to my father that since I started going with her daughter, she had not spent as much time in the house as she had before, and so she wanted my father to make me leave her daughter alone. Instead of having a conversation with me about the woman's complaint, my father ridiculed her in front of his employees. He categorically told her, "My son is a boy, and that there is nothing I can do about this. It is up to your daughter to leave him alone." Because I had more than one girlfriends, my father and his employees thought I was a good catch. Getting the approval

© KONINKLIJKE BRILL NV, LEIDEN, 2020 | DOI: 10.1163/9789004440944_003

of my maleness from my father, brother, and male friends was crucial, for such approval confirmed that I fit in the category of manhood.

I was under the constant surveillance of my father who expected me to "behave like a man." I followed for years the male path he paved for my older brother and me. Whereas I was neither criticized nor looked down upon for having more than one girlfriend, my older sisters were reprimanded for having a boyfriend. After all, I was a boy, and boys are expected to have as many girls as they want. Meanwhile, my father physically hit my sister and threatened to stop supporting her academically if she continued seeing her boyfriend. As predicted by my mother, my father stopped supporting my sister with her education after she finished eighth grade; she continued seeing her boyfriend in secret and my father found out about it. This was a sexist excuse he used to not assume his responsibility as a father.

The truth is that my father did not want to invest in my sister's education for fear that she would get pregnant before graduating high school. Meanwhile, I continued my studies while having three girlfriends, and nobody challenged my male, sexist behavior. I was free to have as many girls as I wanted, for which I always got recognition in my community from my male friends. I could bring girls home, telling my sisters, my older brother and my parents they were my friends, and they would not have a problem with it. My sisters, however, could not dare take such a risk, for they knew they would be severely punished, and their male friends most likely would not be welcome in my house. Only their male cousins and some boys in the neighborhood whom my parents knew were welcome to my house, though with some level of suspicion.

Because of sexism, my sisters' intelligence was sometimes questioned by my father and by some of their male classmates. I also questioned their intelligence until I was embarrassingly confronted by one of my sister's middle school teachers on my poor academic performance in her class. While I was attending the same middle school as my sister, her teacher, who was also my teacher, asked me: "Are you Freda Orelus' brother?" I responded saying yes. She then went on to say, "How come she is a very studious student and you're not? You need to have her help you with your homework; otherwise, you will not pass my class." I knew at the time that my sister was a very good student like the teacher said, and that I was not as focused as she was. However, because of the way I was taught to perceive women's intelligence, I kept denying the fact that my sister was an intelligent woman, and therefore did not take my teacher's warning seriously. As a result, I failed her class and had to repeat it.

Because of my father's constant questioning of my sister's intelligence and refusal to financially and morally support her with her schooling, she ended up dropping out of school. My mother tried hard on her own to help her stay in school, but financially she could not continue to do so. My sister suffered from seizures that my father used as an excuse to discourage my mother from continuing to support her in school. However, the hidden truth behind my father's tactic was that he did not want my mother to invest her money in the education of my sister, assuming that she would get pregnant before finishing high school.

Had my sister been given the same opportunity to receive the same support that I did, she would have finished high school and graduated from college. Because of a lack of opportunity and support from my father, my sister ended up doing the same type of menial job that my mother did for over 40 years, that is, buying and selling goods on the street, while I am now a university professor. Because of a lack of an advanced formal education, my sister's choices were extremely limited. The chances for her to move up the economic, social, and political ladder are extremely slim now, while mine are increasing.

Furthermore, if I were to go back to my early twenties to talk about my immigrant experience, I would have to conclude that my brother and I have been able to immigrate to the U.S. because of our male privileges. As a prime example, when it was time for my mother to help one of her children to come to the U.S. to seek a better life, she was torn between choosing my eldest sister and my older brother. Traditionally, when poor or working class Haitian families are making a sacrifice by selling their lands and/or other assets to send their children overseas legally or "illegally," the eldest child is usually if not always chosen over the younger ones.

In the case of my mother, she was advised by both her male and female friends to choose my older brother over my eldest sister, assuming that my older brother was stronger and more intelligent. I later realized that the decision was gender-biased. One of the arguments that my mother's friends made was that my older brother had a higher level of formal education than my eldest sister. What my mother's female and male friends failed to realize was that my older brother was more advanced in school than my eldest sister because he had more opportunities as a boy than my sister had as a girl. Furthermore, the fact that my sister had fewer years of formal education than my older brother did not necessarily mean that he was smarter than she was. Finally, there was no concrete evidence that my older brother was stronger than my eldest sister.

A fixed expectation that many poor families in the Caribbean have of their children whom they financially help to leave their native land to seek a better life in the U.S. or elsewhere is that in return they will help other siblings to join them once they are established in the foreign land. This was the expectation that my mother, my sisters, father, and I had of my brother. After having lived in the U.S. for five years, my brother sponsored me so I could immigrate here. The hope or, to be precise, the expectation is that by being here I would be able to support family members who were left behind. In all fairness, my brother should have sponsored one of my older sisters to come to the U.S. Instead, I was chosen. Like my brother, my gender worked in my favor. My father and my mother believed that I was the best "candidate" to join my brother in the U.S. supposedly because of my age (even though I was three years younger than the sister that I followed) and my higher level of education than my sisters'. Again, what my family members and my brother's friends grossly failed to understand was that I had a higher level of formal education than my sisters because my father supported me with my schooling while he did not support them.

My maleness allowed me to leave my native land, to attend college, to go to graduate school, and later become a university professor at the expense of my sisters who did not finish high school. In fact, the eldest one did not even attend high school. She was jobless for almost all her adult life and depended on my mother with her two children until she died, even though she supposedly had a husband. My other sister, who is still alive, has been unemployed for several years now and dependent on her Christian and patriarchal husband. He did so by convincing her to quit her little business she had buying and selling goods to merely become a housewife.

Although most women in my neighborhood were hardworking people who worked long hours on the farm, in factories, and in the street selling goods to feed their families, they were not treated with the level of respect and dignity they deserved. Many of them were merely treated as "women," that is, as weak individuals who should not be trusted to make important decisions for the family. Their husbands were the decision makers even though many of these women were the breadwinners in their house.

Let us take the case of my own mother who is the hardest working woman I have ever known. Even though she was an independent woman who put us to school with her sweat and hard work, she always felt that my father had to be the one who decided for the family. It was not until she finally realized that my father was unreliable and irresponsible that she decided to start making some decisions on her own for the family. My father never approved my mother's decisions, which he assumed were not well thought out; he often ridiculed her, especially when she made a decision that he thought was poor, like selling a piece of her land to rent an apartment in Port-au-Prince so my older brother could attend high school.

My mother made that decision for the following reason: there was no high school in the countryside where I was born and partially grew up. Therefore, in order for my older bother to attend high school, we had to move to

Port-au-Prince, a decision that my father rejected because he felt that it was a waste of money to make such a sacrifice. Since my mother did not get any financial support from my father, she decided to sell a piece of her lands so she could rent an apartment for us.

Three years later, we were forced to move back to the countryside because my mother was not able to continue to pay the rent by herself. My father was happy about this, and he ridiculed my mother and my sister, who ended up dropping out of high school. My brother and I were able to move back to Port-au-Prince due to the generosity of some family members who allowed us to stay at their houses. I continued my education while my brother stopped going to school to find ways to financially support himself and the rest members of our family. This was what expected of him as the oldest brother. My sisters stayed in the countryside doing almost nothing.

It is worth noting that I am alluding here mostly to working class Haitian families, including mine, whose realities I am most familiar with. In middle and upper middle class Haitian families, the power relations between men and women might be different though I am convinced sexism has impacted at varying degrees all women in the Caribbean, especially in Haiti where I witnessed its most harmful effect. Before going any further, I wish to pose this question: what is the relevance of these narratives to this book?

Let me try answering this question. The prime reason is that as a Caribbean man who had the opportunity to develop some level of consciousness about my own maleness, I believe that it is critically important to retrace and share my personal experience with sexism, homophobia, and patriarchy to which I was exposed as a child. To fight against sexism, a learned behavior through socialization and from the environment, it is important to start at home, which is often if not always the place where one learns whether to treat women humanely or inhumanly. Home is also a place where one learns the very first notions of how to "be a man," which means for many men of African descent that I interviewed for this book, "be tough," "be aggressive," "don't show any sign of weakness to your friends and enemies."

I am telling these stories because I want to stop being the man that my father wanted me to be, that is, not to show any emotion like crying whether or not I am hurt physically and psychologically; always try to be in control the way he always wanted me to be; and not to waste time consulting women before making a decision because in his view and in the view of many other men in my community they (women) are not mentally and intellectually capable of offering the advice that men need to make an informed decision.

I must confess that even though I refuse to be the man my father and his male employees expected me to be, I have not yet fully transcended my male and sexist behavior and tendencies. I am still struggling to rise above the image and definition of maleness that my father, my close male friends, and other family members passed on to me while growing up. This image is ingrained in my mind to an extent where sometimes I catch myself reproducing some of the sexist behaviors that I witnessed my father displaying at home when I was a child: sexist behaviors such as tacitly expecting my female partner to cook and clean the house. Like my father, sometimes I have expected my female partner to have dinner ready at home for me when I come back home from school or from work. At times, I have been disappointed when I come home and there was no food for me to eat, especially when I knew she was home all day.

Another inherited male behavior that I have been struggling with is my socially constructed belief that I should not cry as a man in front of women or simply not to cry at all because, as I directly or indirectly learned from my father, crying is a sign of weakness. At no time did I see my father cry in front of me, not even when his mother passed away. Following consciously or unconsciously my father's footsteps, I did not cry when he died about 17 years ago. Nor did I ever cry when I was sad or facing hardship both in my personal and professional lives. My female partner, who often expresses her emotions through crying, found it odd. I have evolved since. I now cry in front of her and my children.

Moreover, I have not yet fully outgrown my inner impulsive sexist behavior and old male mentality, which has sometimes led me to romanticize women's beauty and at times look at them as a source of pleasure. Challenging myself to internally change this male behavior has been a terrific psychological battle, but certainly a battle that is worth fighting for, especially for a man like myself who wants to liberate himself from the misconception of maleness that had been passed on to me at a young age. In short, to borrow Bobbie Harro's phrase, I have not yet transcended "the cycle of socialization" in which I was born and grew up. Harro (2000) explains the cycle of socialization in the following terms:

> Our socialization begins before we are born with no choice on our part. No one brings us a survey, in the womb, inquiring into which gender, class, religion, sexual orientation, cultural group, ability status, or age we might want to be born. These identities are ascribed to us at birth through no effort or decision or choice of our own; there is, therefore, no reason to blame each other or hold each other responsible for the identities we have. (as cited in Adams et al., 2000, p. 16)

Harro (2000) is right indeed. To contribute to a society that is equitable and free of gender and sexual oppressions, men, including men of color, need to dismantle the oppressive form of maleness that has been inculcated in our mind and has informed our sexist attitude and behavior toward women. To dismantle this form of maleness, first and foremost we ought to strive to change, or at least challenge, the rules of the patriarchal system. As long as they remain intact are not challenged, women will continue to be victimized by sexism. Even though men of all races have been beneficiaries of sexism, it needs to be acknowledged that they have suffered of it, too. For example, because of this divide, men are socialized to hide their emotion and not to be in touch with their soul.

This is why the fight against sexism or, for that matter, against any form of oppression should not be left only to those who have been victimized and marginalized by it. Those who by accident of birth happen to belong to the privileged race, sex, gender or class have a moral and historical obligation to align themselves with oppressed groups. Only individualistic people who want to continue to live in an isolated island of privileges surrounded by miserable and dark villages where many oppressed have been living can shut the eyes of their conscience to social injustice. This, unfortunately, has been the lifestyle that many privileged and powerful straight men have lived.

Like whiteness, there are a lot of unearned privileges attached to maleness. These unearned privileges are often taken for granted and sometimes abused by those who inherit them. Ironically, people who are the beneficiaries of such privileges often feel they are entitled to them even though they did not have to work hard to earn them. By virtue of one's race/ethnicity, skin tone, sex, gender, and family's social class, one can be born into the world of many privileges to which many people would never have access. Those who happen to be the heirs of unearned and undeserved privileges have rigorously been fighting to maintain them. Though sad, this should not be hard to understand because, as it is often the case, people do not easily give up their privilege regardless of what form it may take.

This logically explains the ever-present need for the marginalized and the disinherited to continue to fight for equal opportunities and resources. However, expecting those who have been marginalized and oppressed – because of their sexual and racial identities, among others – to engage alone in this battle is in itself social injustice, for they have no control over the sex and race in which they were born. They should not be responsible either for the social injustice or for the inequality to which they have been subjected due to their racial and sexual characteristics.

By virtue of my sex (male) and sexual orientation (straight), I have some privileges that women, particularly women of color, as well as bisexual, transgender, and transsexual women and men, do not have. Some of the privileges that I have as a heterosexual man are the following:

QUESTIONING MY BLACK MALE AND HETEROSEXUAL PRIVILEGES

1. Being able to walk on the street late at night without fear of being raped.
2. Working at any male-dominated institution without being fearful about sexual harassment.
3. Not having to be concerned about getting paid a lot less than my co-workers for the same amount and kind of work that I do.
4. Having no doubt that my gender/sex is represented through texts that I read in school, in church, and elsewhere.
5. Running for office without being concerned that my gender might be an issue or obstacle, which can prevent me from getting elected.
6. Not having to speak up all the time so that my voice can be heard.
7. Not feeling that I have to be assertive and vocal so that I will not be invisible in the eyes of some of my male co-workers, colleagues, partners, bosses, friends, and even family members.
8. Not being expected to be silent, merely listen and be talked to, and follow orders from my boss and my spouse.
9. Not being expected to be sexy, slim, and beautiful in order to please my partner, my spouse, or men in general.
10. Not having to constantly fight with my parents who expect me to take care of the domestic chores.
11. Not being offered promotion in exchange of sex.
12. Not having to worry about getting fired because of my refusal to sleep with my boss, or for challenging him.
13. Not being concerned about being a minority at institutions like the army and other key governmental positions.
14. Not being concerned about being beaten by my spouse or partner at home.
15. Cheating on my wife or girlfriend, and having no concern about being called a bitch and looked down upon by my friends and some members of my community.
16. Performing with confidence when I speak in front of people because I know they will most likely believe what I say because I am a man.
17. Not having to worry about being physically hurt and even killed while attempting to have an "illegal abortion," and also not having to deal alone with the physical and emotional pain that results from it.
18. Not having to worry about being told that I am weak, that I am not smart and strong enough to study physics, chemistry, biochemistry, or any other scientific discipline.
19. Not having to be too concerned about being a single parent because my partner can run away and leave me alone with the child or the children that we both brought to this world.
20. Not being afraid that my parents might not invest as much in me as they do in my siblings because of my gender.

28   CHAPTER 2

21. Not being concerned I might be denied the opportunity to play certain sports in which I am interested because of my gender.

22. Not being pressured by family members and my community to stay in an abusive relationship to save face and maintain the family traditions.

23. Not being constantly pressured to find a man, get married in my twenties and have children so I will not be seen as a failure and/or abnormal in the eyes of my family, my community, and society at large.

24. Not having to worry about being harshly criticized for losing my virginity in early teenage years.

25. Not having to worry about being dominated and treated unfairly by my own siblings and parents because of my gender and sex.

26. Not having to worry about being called names like faggot, sissy, or homo.

27. Not being concerned about being fired if my boss finds out that I am not straight.

28. Not having to think about being denied job promotion because of my sexual orientation.

29. Not having to worry about being denied housing because the landlord does not like gay, bisexual, transgender, transsexual, and transgender people.

30. Not being concerned about being murdered on the street and/or by a group of gay haters because of my sexual orientation.

31. Not being forced to move from state to state and/or from city to city to find a place where I can marry the partner that I love and live peacefully as a citizen.

32. Not having to be mistrusted around children, let alone not being allowed to adopt them because of my sexual orientation.

33. Not having to fight constantly with the legal system for equal protections and equal rights because of institutionalized discrimination against people with my sexual orientation.

34. Not having to be concerned for being judged harshly for showing affection to my spouse, girlfriend or partner in public.

35. Not being forced to pretend or perform as straight in front of my parents, friends, and members at my church to protect myself from being chastised, isolated, and singled out.

36. I can run for office and be a part of any institution like the armed forces and the police and not have to worry about anyone discriminating against me because of my sexual orientation.

37. I can be rude and people will not pass judgments based on my sexual orientation and/or call me names.

QUESTIONING MY BLACK MALE AND HETEROSEXUAL PRIVILEGES 29

38. Not having to worry about being unwelcome or discriminated against by my classmates or excluded from certain activities at school because of my sexual orientation.
39. Not having to commit suicide because I am depressed, isolated, and afraid to open up to my parents and friends, telling them that I am different, that I am not the straight person that they assume I am.
40. Not having to be constantly upset when I am watching a show on TV or a movie where they ridicule, infantilize, sexualize, and even objectify people who share the same or similar sexual orientations as mine.

2   Critical Reflection

The list above can be much longer. However, the point that I am trying to make is that as a heterosexual Black man, my gender and sex, situated in the context of the patriarchal system, have afforded me many unearned privileges. At the same time it is imperative that I point out that as a Black man who was born in the Caribbean, who speaks with a "foreign accent" and who did not have access to the same economic, political, and cultural capital as many privileged, straight White men have, I am subject to many forms of the oppressions listed above of which women, particularly women of color, and gay, bisexual, transgender, and transsexual people have been a victim. In other words, classism, racism, sexism, and homophobia are interrelated and therefore should not be analyzed separately; they all need to be part of the larger discussion and analysis about sexism, heterosexism, and other forms of oppression.

For example, the patriarchal world, which has been in existence for centuries, has not impacted White women the same way as women of color. Nor has it benefited Black men to the same degree as White men, especially the privileged ones. Because of the way this patriarchal world was established and run by the White slave masters, many White women had, and continue to have, a lot more privileges than enslaved African men and women. Thus, in the unequal power relation between slaves and non-slaves that shaped the context of sugarcane plantations and cotton fields, gender did not matter much as far as enslaved Black men and White women were concerned. In fact, White women who married wealthy White men owned both female and male slaves and had control over their lives. Federici (2004) noted, "Regardless of their social origin, White women were upgraded or married off within the ranks of the White power structure, and whenever possible they became owners of slaves themselves, usually female ones, employed for domestic work" (p. 108).

By virtue of their skin, both White men and women continue to enjoy in this so-called post-slavery and postcolonial era privileges similar to the ones they had enjoyed during slavery. Although men of color in general have greatly benefited from their maleness, many of them have been in a subordinate position in comparison to some White men and women, with the exception of a few privileged Black men, like former African American President Barack Obama. For example, as a Black man I may have the same level of formal schooling that a White man has; however, by virtue of his whiteness, this White man will most likely have a better chance of access to more opportunities and resources than I. In fact, as historically documented, many men of African descent have been denied positions that are given instead to White men who are less qualified than they are. Similar to White men, White women tend to have more opportunities to fulfill their God-given potential in this society than many women and men of color. If these White women are from privileged backgrounds and highly educated, they tend to have a much better chance of achieving their goals that Black men with similar backgrounds might not be able to achieve because of institutionalized racism. I am fully aware that what I argue above is not the absolute truth as there are a few men of color who have managed to gain a higher status in the political spectrum and at some institutions than White women because of sexism. I argue, however, that many of these Black men have been merely used as tokens by this White patriarchal system, which has been under the ideological, economic, and political control of powerful, conservative White men.

CHAPTER 3

Growing up Poor and Black and Succeeding in an Uneven World

Given my social class background and life trajectory, never in my wildest dream had I thought that someday I would become a university professor in the most powerful country on earth, the United States of America. What do I mean by this statement? Engaging this question requires that I slowly build my arguments by recapturing and describing in detail my Odyssey as a working class Black male who was born, raised, and [mis]educated in a colonial school system in a developing country, and who immigrated to America, where I have known both joy and pain, which I talk about in this chapter and provide more details about in the following chapters. Even though I have achieved both academic and professional successes beyond peers' and relatives' expectations and hidden doubts, and for which I am grateful, I have experienced severe forms of systemic racism in this country, like all Black men and women, and definitely racial micro-aggressions as a Black professor and administrator in the Ivy Halls of White America.

I left Haiti – a country from which I hold tender memories and yet felt uncertain about my future due to political corruption and abject poverty – in my early 20s to immigrate to the United States of America – a country that is full of opportunities and yet plagued with structural racism, xenophobia, and White supremacy, among other social wrongs. Although the youngest child of seven siblings, I was the first one to complete high school at the age of 22, a bachelor's degree at 28, a master's degree at 32, and doctorate degree at 39 qualifying me to become a university professor when I was nearly 40. None of my siblings finished high school, except my brother through a GED. The eldest of my two sisters did not even finish middle school, while the one that I follow dropped out of high school when she was about 16. My mother did not go beyond sixth grade, while my father did not know how to read or write. As for my older brother, he started college with a GED but dropped out and has been since contemplating to return. Last time we spoke about it, he informed me that he was planning on going back to college to pursue a nursing degree.

Given my social class background, I was not expected to attend and finish high school, let alone attend graduate school and become a university professor. Instead, like some of my neighbors, I was expected to follow my father's footsteps to become a carpenter, or else a poor farmer who is forced to sell his

© KONINKLIJKE BRILL NV, LEIDEN, 2020 | DOI: 10.1163/9789004440944_004

labor to a "grandon" (Haitian people who own a lot of lands and have many other assets besides), get a wife and some mistresses, grow old, and die poor. Or, alternatively, I could have become a soldier like my father at one point wished for me, a tailor like some of my neighbors, a bus driver, or a seasonal worker who does manual jobs here and there for survival, like some of the workers who worked on a house I built there from 2014–2015 when I was sabbatical. Or, like thousands of young Haitians, I could have become a gang member or simply a thief who killed people for money or other reasons.

Out of the hundreds of people with whom I grew up, I was one of the few who made it through high school, to which millions of poor Haitians still do not have access. In fact, in some rural areas, including the one where I spent part of my childhood, attending enough school to learn the basic reading and writing skills remains a dream for thousands of poor Haitian children. Some of these children had to labor long hours on farms owned by power brokers who stole lands from poor Haitian peasants; many of them could not afford to send their children to the local school because of financial difficulties. Though I am the youngest in my family, I was the first child to graduate from high school and go to college.

My older sisters were supposed to graduate high school before me but they did not make it beyond eighth grade. My father did not support the idea of investing in my sisters' education, fearing that they would get pregnant before graduating. In fact, my father was not alone in being reluctant to invest in his daughters' education. Many fathers believe that girls should get some basic education and then stay home to help their mother clean, cook, and take care of their younger brothers and sisters. Although this might not reflect the reality of middle and upper middle class Caribbean women, it remains a fact that sexism affects most, if not all, women in the Caribbean.

Although considered late, when I graduated high school, it was a dream come true for my mother who sacrificed everything to support me throughout my high school years. I remember how proud she was to tell her friends, "The last drop (i.e. my youngest son) just graduated from high school." However, the idea of attending college was foreign to my mother who did not go beyond sixth grade. When I told her that I was applying for college, she replied: "I thought you were done with school, my son; when will you be done with school so that you can get a job to help me?" Though disappointed that I was not done yet with school, my mother continued to support me through college hoping that I would find a job after I graduate. Unfortunately, I never got a job like my mother had hoped until after I left the Afro-Caribbean America for the Multiracial and Multilingual United States of America.

GROWING UP POOR AND BLACK AND SUCCEEDING IN AN UNEVEN WORLD 33

My high school and college years within a school system, which is still colonial based, were shadowed by political turmoil that paralyzed the whole country. However, until I became aware of the socio-economic and political challenges my native land was facing, I lived an innocent, naïve, and laissez-faire life style. I did not realize to what extent this country was devastated economically and politically by internal divisions that resulted from bloody fights among leaders in constant fight for power. Nor did I realize to what extent it was also economically and socially deteriorated by imperialist manipulations coming from western countries, such as the United States, France, and Canada.

The reason I lived this innocent and naïve life was that I did not have the political awareness and consciousness to question what I was taught to be natural and canonical truth. Until I started to question the [dis]order of things, I was regarded and treated as a good boy: obedient, smart, and polite. However, when I began asking pertinent or threatening questions about the school system that is colonial-based then, my high school teachers and some of my classmates labeled me as atheist, an angry, a rebel, and a confused boy. In school, my classmates and I were not expected to ask too many independent-minded questions that would oblige our teachers to tell us the truth, or challenge them to help us answer the following questions:

- Why do students living in formerly colonized countries have to use textbooks and colonial masterpieces whose content is culturally and historically alienating to them?
- Why is French the primary language of instruction in school but not Creole, our native language?
- Why are professors who always speak French and English in class are considered "smart," "sharp," and "stylish," whereas those who dare use Creole as the instructional language are considered less intelligent by students, colleagues, and even by the school principal?

What has been happening in the school system of neocolonized countries is not as prevalent as to what occurred in colonial school systems during colonization. However, it is undeniable that the educational legacy of colonialism continues impacting the school system of countries such as Haiti, India, and Tanzania. For example, in Haiti, even after 200 years of independence, the language of the French colonizers is still valued over the Haitian native language, Creole. When I was in middle school and high school (from mid 1980s to early 1990s), all of the textbooks that I had to use for class were in French. Nowhere in these textbooks, either on the cover or inside, were there pictures that reflected the reality of Haiti. These textbooks were and perhaps still are a reflection of the cultural and historical realities of France, realities to which Haitian students like myself could not relate.

As a result, a great number of Haitian students, including myself, felt linguistically and culturally homeless because there was no connection between what we read in these textbooks and our culture. In fact, as a high school student I always felt foreign and culturally and historically alienated reading stories in these textbooks, whose cultural and historical baggage was irrelevant to my lived experience. Not being able to see myself culturally and historically through school materials that my teacher used in class led me to resist what he taught in class. This also led me to question my Mathematics teacher's attitude towards the French language and culture. This teacher always took pride in recounting how well French educators trained him to become a Math teacher at a French Teachers Training Program in Haiti. At no time did he ever use in class a single word of Creole, the language I knew best as a working class student. Instead, he seemed to take pride in using French as the language of instruction.

Moreover, throughout my high school experience in Haiti, I was never encouraged by my teachers to challenge and try to deconstruct the hidden ideology embedded in the French textbooks that I was required to use in class. On the contrary, what I witnessed and personally experienced was that teachers were not only complacent about teaching French literature and history, but they also took pride in repeating, like parrots, to students their pre-fabricated knowledge about these subjects. At no time, did I recall my high school teachers attempting to question and challenge old French values, beliefs, and ideology entrenched in French textbooks that were imposed on them to use in class. Consequently, Haitian students, including myself, spent years from elementary to middle and high schools absorbing information that had no meaning to our lives. In fact, information acquired from these French textbooks structured my mind, to a great extent, to accept passively and reproduce the false idea that France is Haiti's mother country and source of knowledge.

After years of indoctrination, I became a docile reproducer of French values, beliefs, and cultural norms. For instance, until I developed critical consciousness, I used to believe that the French language and literature were better than Creole and the Haitian literature. As a result, through social interaction I always used French, the language of the colonizer, to communicate with and impress people, rather than Creole, my native tongue. What I was not aware of, then, as Wane (2006) notes, was that:

> The use of a foreign language as a medium of education makes a child foreign within her or his own culture, environment, etc. This creates a colonial alienation. What is worse, the neocolonized subject is made to

GROWING UP POOR AND BLACK AND SUCCEEDING IN AN UNEVEN WORLD   35

see the world and where she or he stands in it as seen, and defined by or reflected in the culture of the language of imposition. This is made worse when the neocolonized subject is exposed to images of her or his world mirrored in the written language of her or his colonizer, where the natives' language, cultures, history, or people are associated with low status, slow intelligence, and barbarism. (p. 100)

Wane's remark speaks directly to my schooling experience in Haiti. Reflecting on that experience, I have come to understand that teachers or students, who lack historical and cultural consciousness, sometimes let themselves get trapped in the linguistic oppression of the colonizers, who always expect the colonized to speak the colonial language at the expense of their own. This sad experience with my Math teacher, more importantly, helped me better understand that the school system of a country constitutes its ideological apparatus. Therefore, if any radical social, cultural, and political changes are to occur, it must begin in the school system that has been historically used to maintain and/or challenge the status quo. It goes without saying that the school system can be a dangerous institution that reproduces the dominant ideology and/ or a site of struggle where ideological and political fights for a just and democratic society can take place.

Furthermore, looking back at my schooling experience in Haiti, I now realize how sad it is that most of my high school classmates were more knowledgeable about French literature and history than they were about Haitian literature and culture. This is precisely what happened to colonized people during colonization. The colonized was more knowledgeable about the culture and history of the colonizer than their own. However, this did not happen in a vacuum. The colonized, through schooling, were taught that their indigenous knowledge was barbarous, uncivilized, and therefore was worthless in comparison to the European-based knowledge and formation they were receiving in school.

The Haitian school system that I knew as a high school student was set up in a way that failed Haitian students both culturally and historically. In other words, this school system graduated students who might not have had a clear sense of their history and culture. Hence, locating this form of mis-education that my classmates and I experienced in a global educational context, I ask: what can be expected of a generation that does not to have a sound understanding of its own history and culture? I go further asking: what should educators do to ensure that the school system of their countries is not a duplicate of the old colonial school system and/or the western neoliberal educational policies?

Why do western imperialist powers always feel they have to intervene in times of "political crisis" in Third World countries and try to control the internal political affair of these countries? Why are farmers discouraged to grow rice, corn, and beans because of an overflow of these products in their native land imported from the West? Spending about three semesters in college in my native land did not enable me to develop a critical mind so I could answer the questions posed above. My mis-education failed me on gender and social class issues, among others.

1   My *Mis-Education*

My high school and college experiences did not help me develop critical aware-ness to challenge the patriarchal system. Let me explain. Throughout my high school and college years in Haiti, I never came across a teacher who discussed and interrogated anything related to sexist and homophobic practices. Although gender was part of the class dynamic in that boys were expected to be smarter than girls and be a lot more advanced in science than girls, none of my teachers ever brought the gender issue to the fore of classroom discussions. As a case in point, when a girl made first or second honor, this was always a surprise to many people, including male teachers who expected boys to be on top of the list of highly achieving students. Male students who were not good at math, physics, or chemistry were sometimes looked down upon and ridiculed by their female and male classmates and their teachers. Many of my female classmates internalized the myth that men are biologically and mentally wired to be better at science than girls. One of my close female high school class-mates and friends, Dorval Marie Gaelle, sometimes made fun of me because she was a lot more advanced in math, chemistry, and physics than I was.

In fact, she once made me feel embarrassed when she, three of my male classmates, and I were trying to solve some problems in our physics and math textbooks. She said to me, "What happens to you, Wilbert? How come you don't know how to solve these problems?" I was embarrassed in front of my male friends and also felt that my maleness was questioned and threatened for not being able to solve a math problem that my female classmate was able to solve. This experience troubled me psychologically for years. Even now when a woman approaches me and asks me to help her solve a math problem and I find myself unable to do so; it triggers the inadequacy about my maleness that I felt when I could not solve the math problems that Dorval expected me to.

In my history classes, my teachers, who were mostly males, constantly referred to male heroes such as Toussaint L'Ouverture, Jean Jacques Dessalines

GROWING UP POOR AND BLACK AND SUCCEEDING IN AN UNEVEN WORLD   37

and Henry Christophe who fought for the independence of Haiti. Heroines like Defile who played a very significant role in our historical life were rarely mentioned. No names of the female slaves who helped these male heroes in their bloody fight against the French colonizers were ever mentioned in my history classes, as if these men fought this fight alone. It was in my Haitian and French literature classes, where I learned about French and Haitian male writers such as Victor Hugo, Jean Jacques Rousseau, Oswald Durand, Etzer Vilaire, Frederic Marcelin, Luis Joseph Janvier, Anténor Firmin, Jean Price Mars, Jacques Roumain, and Jacques Stephen Alexis. These male writers were, and still are, to some extent my role models. In other words, they left great scholarly work and a glorious historical legacy I have been looking up to. Some of them, like Anténor Firmin, Jacques Stephen Alexis, and Jean Price Mars, have influenced my thinking. Although there were, and there are many still, incredible female Haitian writers, like Mirlande Manigat, I did not know much about them, for my history and literature teachers rarely mentioned their names in class. Nor was I encouraged by my older male friends and mentors to explore the scholarly work of female Haitian writers.

I did not feel the incentive to take the initiative to explore their work, for my maleness was represented through my history and literature textbooks. When I had to refer to my ancestors I did not have to worry about using both subject pronouns "he" and "she." I was directly or indirectly taught to use only "he," for it was the universal pronoun that was used throughout my history and literature textbooks and classroom discussions to refer to those who shaped my historical and cultural lives. I was misled to believing that they were all males. The subject pronoun "she" was excluded from my vocabulary when I was talking or asked to talk about those who sacrificed their lives for the independence of the land where I was born, and Haitian writers who produced great scholarly work.

What about my high school and college female classmates? What did they have in terms of female role models? There were certainly many Haitian female historical figures, but they were unknown to many of the students due to the fact that the education they received was gender biased. Many of my female classmates were brainwashed to accept the lack of recognition of female heroines' contribution to the Haitian literature and history. This distortion of historical facts was reinforced by the dynasty of Haitian male presidents and governmental officials who have controlled the political, educational, and the economic arenas for decades. My former female high school and college classmates and other women have continued to witness the perpetuation and normalization of maleness in Haiti despite a short-lasting shift in the political paradigm that took place with the emergence of Ertha Pascal Trouillot. Former

Judge Trouillot became the first acting Haitian female President from 1990 to 1991 as a result of political turmoil that destroyed the country.

All in all, my colonial based schooling experience did not enable me either to understand the western cultural, political, and economic assaults against developing countries. I had to dig into the works of authors, such as Frantz Fanon, Albert Memmi, and Ngugi Wa Thiong'o, among others, to critique what I was not allowed to know and question, that is, my mis-education. Due to my early mis-education, I was ignorant of the interference of western countries in political affairs of Third World countries and the continued negative effects of colonialism on these countries. My high school and college experiences in a colonial-based school system did not teach me either that growing up in an uneducated and poor family should not dictate one's destiny. Nor did these experiences teach me that being poor should not prevent one from questioning why Third World countries have been put in a political and economic situation where they always have to rely on the western world for foreign aid or, worse yet, borrow money from IMF and the WB with exorbitant rates. Nor did my high school diploma and the semesters at the Haitian State University equip me with the necessary critical and political consciousness to understand why factory workers worked long hours making shirts, pants, jackets, shoes, baseball, and football equipment for corporate capitalist interests while they could not feed or clothe their children, let alone send them to school.

I remember my neighbors and relatives having to work ten to twelve hours a day, and yet they frequently had to borrow money from other neighbors and family members to feed their children and pay their bills. Selling their labor force for hours in foreign-owned assembly plants did not enable them to improve their living conditions. On the contrary, these conditions had gotten worse from weeks to weeks until they were sent home after the closure of these assembly plants. Even though I was then a young boy, it was not too hard for me to make sense of their miserable conditions. Their tired and ill looking face combined with their sad stories about their job's working conditions were the vivid testimony of their miserable lived experience.

While residing in Haiti, life at times felt rather depressing. In specific terms, while the present did not feel as hopeful, the future, to a great extent, felt bleak. Hence, having the possibility to leave my native land for a multiracial, multicultural, and multilingual land, like the United States of America, was appealing. Indeed, as the United Stated was sold to me as the panacea, moving to this country felt like a safe heaven. I particularly bought in an idealistic view of America because, while growing up in Haiti, poverty was my reality. I wanted to escape a slow death resulting abject poverty and political corruption. Hence, when my brother told me that I could work while getting an education, if I immigrated to the United States, he gave much hope and, most importantly, sparked much enthusiasm and determination in me to leave Haiti for the western world

As a high school student, I detested school, which entailed rote memorization of texts and taking standardized tests. However, I never questioned the high intrinsic value of education and ongoing learning, which I did not, and still do not, necessarily believe is merely the product of a series of letters called PhD, although it is worth pursuing one. I believe that learning particularly occurs through exploration of novel ideas beyond the school walls, through reading and dialogue with people who are different and who, therefore, might have opposing views on issues that we dearly embrace and cherish.

2 Conclusion

To sum it up, my life story is an ontological journey from the first independent Black republic in the western hemisphere, which has unfortunately been impoverished by internal corruption as well as by the geopolitical domination and economic exploitation of western power, to the multiracial, multilingual, multicultural, and multi-historical of the United States of America. In my birth land, I essentially knew only one race, one culture, and one history, whereas in the United States of America, where I have lived the longest, I have known multiple races, cultures, and histories. Due to systemic oppression, namely racism, some of these races, cultures, and histories have been acknowledged and even glorified in schools, the media, and the larger American society, whereas others have been documented through a footnote, or falsified, if not altogether erased, in these institutions. Nonetheless, since I have moved to the United States, I have become a much richer person culturally and linguistically, and I have succeeded academically and professionally while continuing to face and stand up courageously against systemic racism, White supremacy, and xenophobia.

CHAPTER 4

Belonging Neither Here nor There

In this chapter, I build from my experiences growing up in Haiti previously articulated in the preceding chapters to situate the context in which I immigrated to the United States. Specifically, I examine how I was racially, linguistically, and socio-economically positioned in my native land, and in what ways and to what degree my racial, linguistic, and cultural repertoires have been perceived, redefined, and even petrified within the context of the United States. To this end, I explore to what extent those in hegemonic positions of power have constructed my race, nationality, and culture with their implicit historical, and cultural biases and prejudices. And in an attempt to challenge the unequal power relations that often lead to inequities, I use both my "Third World" and western experiences to position myself, establishing what Foucault (1995) calls self-to-self and self-to-others relations. I further explain how I have negotiated this position. To avoid representing myself as a victim, I acknowledge and interrogate my class and male privileges as a Black heterosexual and able-bodied university professor. In short, I situate my story in the larger U.S. context, where people of color have faced many systemic challenges, including racial and linguistic discrimination, and yet have succeeded somehow.

1 I Am My Identities

Some have argued that identity is the reflection of one's sense of self. In this book, I expand upon that premise, examining it from a socially, culturally, and cross-border perspective. One's identity necessarily encompasses one's social, historical, and cultural growth and characteristics (Appiah, 2005; Castells, 2006; Holland, 2003; Morrell, 2015, 2018; Norton, 2000). Understood as such, identity is not static; it is fluid and dialectical. Furthermore, identity is contextual, connected to time. Hence, as one's social, cultural, or political milieu changes, identity evolves in tandem.

This is irrefutably true in my experience: Since I immigrated to the United States in the mid 1990s, my identity has evolved tremendously. Specifically, it has profoundly shifted from being Haitian to being Black, a foreigner, and "an alien" – identifying constructs that persist even as I have become a naturalized U.S. citizen and university professor in an academy where I often feel like a "minority within minorities" (Montero-Sieburth, 2000, p. 228). That is, I have

© KONINKLIJKE BRILL NV, LEIDEN, 2020 | DOI: 10.1163/9789004440944_005

often, if not always, been the only Black male professor in institutions where I have worked, including the current one where I served as the first Black department chair in the history of the school, and the first one in the entire university who was not born in the United States.

By saying that I often feel like a "minority within minorities," I do not intend to fall into victim and self-pity category kind of persons; nor am I seeking compassion, empathy, or sympathy from anyone. It is not my goal either to represent myself here as the "oppressed," as Freire (1993) brilliantly described in his classic *Pedagogy of the Oppressed*, or a victim of a system that often silences the voice of "the subaltern" (Spivak, 1988), and denies them the space needed for themselves and in which they can affirm their multiple identities. The reason I refuse to represent myself as a victim is that, although I have experienced racism, White supremacy, and xenophobia in American society and the academy because of my racial and linguistic backgrounds and country of origin, I am also fully cognizant of unearned privileges to which I have had access as an educated, heterosexual Black male professor, as already noted in the previous chapters.

It is particularly imperative that I highlight this fact because, as noted earlier, while growing up in Haiti, I did not have access to many of the resources that I have had in the United States. My time in Port-au-Prince granted me the opportunity to witness the negative effects of the western form of globalization on Haiti's economic and political system. Because of the overwhelming flow of exported products from western countries, the farmers lost the incentive to grow, for example, organic local corn, beans, rice, and other types of crops, as their value was drastically decreased. The imported products were a lot cheaper than the ones Haitian farmers produced under extreme circumstances – their work was made extremely difficult by an insufficient water supply and a lack of proper irrigation or access to adequate tools. Haitian farmers were not alone facing the challenges that came along with the overflow of western-imported products. Haitian tailors, too, could no longer compete with second-hand imported clothes that invaded the Haitian market. These clothes cost a lot less than the traditional clothing made by tailors. As a result, the poor Haitians had no choice but to purchase what was cheaper and available on the market.

Given the socioeconomic conditions in Haiti and the political instability and internal corruption that have devastated this country since its independence in 1804, I could not think of a better option than leaving my native land for the United States, despite its natural beauty and the sense of community that I truly enjoyed and cherished. Like many immigrants, especially immigrants of color from impoverished countries, I felt that immigrating to the United

States was my only escape from abject poverty, which felt like at times a slow death. However, I am preoccupied with seeking answers to certain questions: What is the cost of leaving my native land to move to the United States, leaving behind loved ones whose lives have gotten worse while mine has improved since? Hasn't the daily price of experiencing racism, xenophobia, linguicism, and White supremacy been heavier than the abject poverty to which I was subject in Haiti? I've been asking myself these puzzling questions for the last two decades or more, since I immigrated to the United States. I will shed light on them in the sections that follow through the recollection and critical reflections of precious memories.

2 Recollecting Precious Memories

I experienced many precious things in my birth land that I have cherished to this day. For example, I enjoyed a sense of community, which often seems lacking here in the United States. Moreover, I was untouched by racism and xenophobia. Furthermore, the concept of racial minority, of which I became fully aware and which forcibly became part of my social and racial identity in the United States, was not part of my vocabulary in Haiti. Oliva Espín (1997) had a similar experience as an immigrant. As soon as she set foot in the United States, Espín (1997) was labeled as minority, although in her country of origin, she was part of the majority. Espín (1997) lamented, "This transition forced me into a minority person's experience, for in the United States being a Hispanic person has very specific emotional, social and identity implications that I had not confronted before" (p. 6). Similarly, in an interview that I had with a noted professor of color, Zeus Leonardo (2011), he critically reflected on and shared how he has been perceived and labeled since he immigrated to the United States from the Philippines. Leonardo (2011) stated he has been mistaken for a Latino, although he does not even speak Spanish. People perceived him as such apparently because of his ethnic and racial characteristics. Leonardo (2011) also talked about various forms of racial challenges he has experienced as a minority professor.

In the context of Haiti, the word "minority," taken literally, could apply to mulatto Haitians, given that they constitute approximately 5 percent of the Haitian population. However, this label has not been placed on them. Like all countries, Haiti is not a homogenous or an equitable country. Factors, such as social class, gender, language, and political corruption cause divisions among Haitians. For example, there is a huge social-class gap between the Haitian bourgeois and the impoverished Haitians, which cannot be ignored. The super-rich Haitians are able to send their children to private schools abroad to study. They have access to private healthcare, and are living in safe or relatively safe neighborhoods. In sharp contrast, the marginalized ones can barely feed themselves, and they tend to live in unsafe neighborhoods, adding to the lack of healthcare and financial constraints that make it a challenge for them to send their children to school. Likewise, female Haitians, especially the poor ones, are not on an equal footing with male Haitians because of patriarchy and sexism. It is much worse for Haitian gays and lesbians who are, in my view, the most oppressed groups. Equally problematic and divisive is the language question in Haiti.

For instance, French, the imposed language of the French colonizer, is valued over Haitian Creole. Because of this colonial legacy, those who speak only Creole – the vast majority of whom tend to be the poor – are looked down upon and have very limited access, if any, to sociopolitical mobility in Haiti. On the other hand, the middle- and upper-class Haitians who have embraced and mastered the French language have historically been the ones dominating Haiti's economic and political systems.

Along the same lines, it is worth noting that the French spoken by poor working-class Haitians does not hold the same social-class status as the French spoken by those who belong to the middle or upper class, especially those who have been privileged enough to study abroad in French-speaking countries such as France, Canada (Montreal), and Belgium. To further complicate the language issue in Haiti, it is equally important to mention that some level of linguistic discrimination based on accents sometimes happens among poor urban and rural working-class Haitians. Depending on the regions they are from, some Haitian's French or Creole accent may be different. Those who believe they speak French or French Creole with the "right accent," meaning close to the Parisian accent, sometimes assume they are linguistically superior to, or more sophisticated than, those who do not.

Hence, compared to the category of marginalized Haitians mentioned above, I was and am still somewhat privileged. Despite my humble working-class background, I was fortunate to attend college in Haiti and consequently had the opportunity to learn and speak fluent French – the language of the Haitian dominant class. In addition, I have my male and heterosexual privileges, which have protected me from sexual and homophobic oppressions that many female and queer Haitians have to face in their daily lives – though because of one's gender or sexual expression, one can be a victim of homophobia. Because of these privileges, in Haiti I could comfortably mingle and interact with other Haitians in my community without being constantly reminded by their words, deeds, or behavior of my racial, linguistic, and sexual identities.

At no time was I ever concerned that one might think I was hired at a position for which I am highly qualified because of my race, to fill a government-mandated quota for affirmative action.

However, immediately after I immigrated to the U.S., all these privileges – the sense of community and mental tranquility regarding racial and linguistic issues that I personally enjoyed in Haiti – disappeared. In a country that takes pride in calling itself democratic and wants to be a model for the world, it is ironic that certain groups have been stereotypically and prejudicially labeled and therefore treated as the "other." This violates the very idea that this country is democratic. Therefore, we must also ask, are we truly living in a democratic country? If so, for whom has this country been a democratic country?

In my view, using people's racial, ethnic, and cultural backgrounds and country of origin to label them as the "other" is a direct assault on the spirit and fundamental ideas that inform a democratic society. In a democratic society, there should be space for people to affirm their identities and be active participants in the political decision-making process; people should not be passive spectators of this process. I argue that in a democratic society, people should not ever feel that their race, culture, native tongue, and or nationality is a problem or mere looked down upon. Furthermore, in a democratic country, those in power should not purposely attribute negative labels to marginalized groups so they can treat them as the "wretched of the earth" (Fanon, 1963). Unfortunately, this has been happening in this country, and it has served particularly the interests of those who have benefited from privileges attached with Whiteness. The noble idea of democracy needs to be a reality not only for those who happen to be embodied in the "right" skin, who speak the English language with the "right accent," and belong to the dominant class, but also for those who may not fit these labels.

3   Coping with Bitter and Sweet Feelings Living in the United States

Both bitter and sweet feelings overcast my life journey to the U.S. diaspora, similar to what W. E. B. Du Bois (1995) called double consciousness. Despite the challenges mentioned above, I must admit that this country has enabled me to accomplish many amazing things, such as having the opportunity to earn a doctorate degree that qualified me to become a university professor. However, fulfilling the requirements to become a university professor has been in some way coincidental. Given my family background and the painful experiences of my early years, never in my wildest dreams would I have thought that someday I would be a university professor in a country considered the most powerful on earth. I have been fortunate to meet professors who believed in me, mentored me, and strongly encouraged and inspired me to attend graduate school to earn a doctorate degree.

Living in the United States has given me the opportunity to be exposed to multiple cultures that have widened my view of the world. Interacting with individuals from varying cultural, linguistic, historical, social class, and religious backgrounds has helped me become more accepting and tolerant of others and more open-minded than before I immigrated here. This experience has also taught me that the world can be a better place if one gets out of one's skin to make an effort to socialize with and get to know the "other." Knowing the "other" might enable one to challenge old assumptions and learned stereotypes and prejudices that one holds against other peoples and cultures. In short, my experience living in the U.S. diaspora has helped me become more human and culturally richer than I was 20 years ago or so.

On the other hand, like many involuntary immigrants, I feel trapped living here. I feel trapped because I was forced to flee my country, which could have been politically and economically stable had it not been economically destroyed by unfair trade and the corruption of many Haitian presidents (Farmer, 2003). I also am particularly embittered by the U.S. capitalist system which, via the corporate media, keeps feeding me the false hope and illusion that I can "make it" if I work hard enough.

I was overworked and yet underpaid in multiple settings: (1) as a housekeeper and dishwasher in nursing homes and hotels where I spent long hours cleaning, sweeping floors, and washing dishes; (2) as a valet parker at a five-star hotel located in Boston, Massachusetts, where I sometimes stood in the cold to welcome upper-class guests and park and retrieve their fancy cars; (3) as a case manager at a social-service institution in Summerville, Massachusetts, where I helped the elderly meet their needs; (4) and as a teacher in the most marginalized high school in Boston, where I helped immigrant students learn the English language and improve their reading, writing, and critical thinking skills. I still did not "make it." Even though my social-class status has changed by virtue of being a university professor and I have benefited from the privileges that come with such a status, I often have to manage life on a strict budget in order to ensure financially we do not go bankrupt.

My current status as a university professor is not the same as that of impoverished and marginalized groups who have been giving their sweat and blood in factories, for example, and yet are still lagging in this "land of opportunity." One must ask then what excuse the dominant class uses to justify the too-infrequent success of factory workers. Have they not worked hard enough giving their blood for the economic stability of this country? What about the poor immigrants, including Mexican immigrants? Are they not overworked, underpaid, and exploited picking strawberries in California-a state that once belonged to their native country Mexico but was stolen from them after the Mexican-American war-, working long hours in factories, and fighting and dying in wars for the prosperity of this country and in the interest of the dominant class?

4   Awareness as Liberation

Despite the influence of the corporate media, which has been trying to control my mind to make me believe that everything in the West is beautiful, I constantly have to remind myself of my past and present situations, so that I will not be caught up in my comfort zone here. I refuse to forget that there are millions of human beings like me, both in the United States and in developing countries who (1) are homeless; (2) do not have access to clean and safe water; (3) are dying of hunger and curable diseases, such as tuberculosis; (4) are oppressed, tortured, and killed by their own governments, which are often supported by the West (Chomsky, 1994, 2004; Zinn, 2003); (5) do not have access to basic literacy skills, such as being able to read the instruction of their medications (Kozol, 1986, 1992; Mayo, 2017); and (6) have to move from city to city and from refugee camp to refugee camp to avoid the danger of losing their lives, as the result of western invasion and occupation of their countries, or ethnic/tribal conflicts that have ravaged their countries. Sudan, particularly in Darfur, Iraq, and Afghanistan are cases in point.

Growing up, I used to believe that poor people were responsible for their own poverty, and that anyone can become prosperous if he or she works hard enough. In other words, I naively believed in what many Americans believe in: meritocracy. As it is commonly defined, a meritocratic system is one in which those who work hard move ahead and succeed, while those who do not work hard enough remain at a stagnant stage in their economic, social, and even political development. How about marginalized groups, such as Native Americans, African Americans, Latino/as, gays, and poor Whites, who are as determined and driven as I am, who have worked as hard as I have, and who may be as smart, if not smarter than I am, and yet have not been able to achieve the fabled American dream? Was it their fault for not moving up the socioeconomic and political ladder? Or is their lack of "success" due to systemic economic and racial inequality that allows a few to succeed while keeping many in a stagnant state of misery and abject poverty?

As much as those in power want me to embrace the dominant ideology informing the meritocratic system, I must reject it, because I do not believe

BELONGING NEITHER HERE NOR THERE

this system works for the majority of those that have been historically pushed to the margin and placed at the "bottom of the well" (Bell, 1992). Moreover, despite the widespread belief that the United States of America is a land of opportunity, I remain convinced that unequal distribution of resources and wealth has made this idea problematic. This is not to suggest that there are not opportunities here – there are. However, we need to ask, who has access to these opportunities, how and why? We also need to ask why some people have access to certain privileges while others do not.

My experience as a Black male professor and intellectual has forced me to critically reflect on my racial identity and social-class location as well as those of others. For instance, one's racial, linguistic, and social-class backgrounds can allow one certain privileges in a given society. However, these same backgrounds in different political and sociocultural contexts can constitute an obstacle to gaining access to certain positions, particularly in a White male-dominated country like the U.S. To illustrate the point, let's take the example of a person of color who immigrates to another country. This person may have been highly respected and professionally well accomplished in his or her native land. However, because of his/her racial and linguistic backgrounds, he/she may be subject to being treated as a second-class citizen in the foreign land.

For instance, while growing up in Haiti, I never knew what it meant to be a Black and to be treated as such. I have been experiencing blackness since I have moved to the United States. I have been preoccupied by it, and have become self-conscious of my racial identity because of the way I have been treated. While sometimes I have felt invisible, at other times I've felt really visible in the eyes of many because of my blackness. For example, I feel visible because of it when I am walking on the street and a White person fearfully and suddenly distances him or herself from me for fear of being robbed or physically attacked. Also, I felt visible when, on my way back home from school on a Thursday afternoon in 1994, a White police officer followed me, pulled me, handcuffed me, put me in his car, took me to a police station, and detained me for hours for no apparent valid reason.

When I asked the police officer why he pulled me over, he could not give me a clear explanation. Instead, he asked why my eyes were so red, to which I replied saying, "it has been a long day for me officer at school, and I am exhausted. This is why my eyes are red." He dismissed what I told him, saying, "I have been busy all day, too, and my eyes are not red." I remained quiet for a while and then protested by saying, "Are you arresting me because I am Black?" He pretended that he did not hear what I said, and asked, "What did you say? Anything you say can be used against you."

I was frightened by his reaction, so I remained quiet until we reached the police station, where I was detained for about 6 hours with no clear explanation given to me or my brother who came to see me. While I was waiting for my older brother, whom I called to come and bail me out, the police officer was searching my wallet without any warrant, and he completely emptied it. Because I was still learning the English language and I spoke it with a different accent-having been here in the U.S. for about a year-, the police officer suspected that perhaps I was an "illegal" immigrant. I overheard him calling INS (now called Homeland Security) to check on my legal status. Although I was not yet a legal resident, I was allowed to live legally here, so the officer was not successful with his xenophobic plan to spy on me and have me deported.

When my brother came to the police station upset inquiring why I was stopped, arrested, and detained, the police officer replied that I was speeding. My brother replied saying, "Why did not you just give a ticket? Why is he here?" The police responded that I did not stop on time when he pulled me over and that I stopped on the wrong side of the road, which he stated posed a danger to the life of other drivers and passengers. I did stop on side of the road, but I do not recall stopping on the wrong side when he pulled me over. What the police failed to tell my brother was that when he pulled me over, I stayed calm in my car. But he still called for backups and did not ask me why it took me too long to stop when he pulled me over.

Instead, he asked me why the driver's door of my car was damaged and if it was mine, even though he already had in his hands my driver's license and the car's registration clearly indicating that was my car. Finally, the police did not tell my brother that he pressured me to tell him why my eyes were red and that he forcibly pulled me out of the car, forced my head against his car, and he handcuffed me. My brother left the police station extremely upset, and I was still awfully frightened trying to grab my head around the reason(s) why the police treated me the way he did. I soon realized that my Black skin and accent were the two visible markers, which led to my unfair arrest and detention.

In *Black Skin, White Masks*, Frantz Fanon (1967) recounted a similar experience he had in France with a White boy and his mother while walking in the street. The White boy, who seemed to be scared of Fanon's Blackness, fearfully called his mother while pointing to Fanon and said: "Look at the nigger! ... Mama, a Negro! ... Hell, he's getting mad .... Take no notice, sir, he does not know that you are as civilized as we ..." (p. 113).

As Fanon's experience with the White boy and his mother illustrates, one's dark, or Black skin often makes one become a target. Moreover, depending on the context, one's skin tone might make one visible or invisible. For instance, while walking in the street in France, Fanon's skin tone made him become visible in the White little boy's eyes. Similarly, in Belchertown, Massachusetts, where I lived for about a year, I witnessed the nervousness and fear in my White

BELONGING NEITHER HERE NOR THERE

neighbors' faces each time I opened the main entrance door to enter the building where I lived. The most frustrating experience I had living there was when two of my White neighbors completely ignored me when all I wanted to say to them was: "Good morning. How are you today?" At first, I thought they didn't respond because they did not hear me. So the following day, as I was leaving the building, I greeted them while they were standing by the entrance door. They once more ignored me, turning their faces away. They did so as if I were a scary alien invading their "White world." It didn't take me long to realize that despite my genuine smile and politeness, my skin color and possibly my "foreign accent" may have scared them and consequently made them ignore me.

Moreover, the attitude and action of some Belchertown police, who often followed me when I was driving, confirmed my assumption that in my White neighbors' eyes and the eyes of the police, I did not belong in their "White" town. Moving from Belchertown to Amherst, Massachusetts, which was more racially diverse, I thought the White police officers wouldn't act the same way; as it turned out, I experienced the same kind of racial profiling in Amherst as I did in Belchertown. For example, I fooled myself into believing that as a doctoral student living on campus, I would be safe from racial profiling. What I failed to realize was that being a visible Black student at the University of Massachusetts at Amherst is not the same as being a White student there. When I was driving, my status as a doctoral student could not stop a police officer from racially profiling me.

Not only was I racially profiled as a doctoral student but also as an instructor. For example, while teaching an undergraduate course called Foundations of Critical Thinking at a small liberal-art college in western Massachusetts, I was followed by one of the college security guards as if I were a criminal. As I was returning a TV I had used in class – ironically, to show a short documentary on the intersection of race, gender, and social class – to the computer laboratory, a security guard followed me. When I asked him if there was anything wrong, he merely replied, "Sir, I am just doing my job." Doing his job evidently meant keeping an eye on every step that I made as the only Black instructor with a "foreign" accent teaching at that college.

It is worth noting that many other professors of color have also been victims of racial profiling. The arrest of acclaimed Harvard Professor Henry Louis Gates by Sergeant James Crowley in 2009 is a case in point. Crowley arrested Gates after a woman called 911 to report that two men were trying to break into a house. Crowley responded to the call, and as he was trying to locate the suspected burglars, he stepped on the porch of the house where Professor Gates lives, knocked on his door, and asked him to step out. Professor Gates apparently challenged the officer, who arrested him for disorderly conduct.

From the constant racial harassment of White police officers and other White individuals, I inferred that my Black skin must be the factor that has made me become a target and part of the forcibly racialized category of the "other." Consequently, regardless of my social class status as a university professor, my positive attitude, good personality, politeness, high ambition, and inner drive to succeed in life and contribute to society, I have been racially targeted. However, despite the racial experiences noted above, I have tried to do "the right thing"; that is, to be responsible, to obey the law, to show respect to others, and contribute to society through hard work. In other words, I have tried to be what is commonly defined as a "good citizen." However, being a good citizen has not saved me from receiving ill treatment from others, as the examples above illustrate. As Frantz Fanon (1963) wrote: "I am given no chance. I am overwhelmed from without. I am the slave not of the 'idea' that others have of me but of my own appearance" (p. 116).

Since I immigrated to the U.S., I have felt that my racial and linguistic identities and human dignity have been constantly under attack. As I have experienced xenophobia, linguicism, and racism here in this country, the message coming from the U.S. diasporic world has become clear to me: If you do not look like us, do not sound like us, you cannot be a part of us. Like Fanon, "all I wanted was to be a man among other men" (p. 112). But this world has insulted my humanity by looking down upon my racial and linguistic backgrounds.

As a professor of color, not only have I experienced systemic racism and White supremacy but also xenophobia-I have been subject to people's xenophobic attitudes These attitudes come from both students and colleagues, who seem to find it hard to believe that a Black man with a noticeable "foreign accent" can be their professor. Their comments and questions sometimes make me feel that they equate my accent to a lack or a lower level of intelligence. For example, after I formally introduce myself in class, I had an undergraduate student who asked me, in a surprised tone of voice, "Are you really the professor?" I overheard students asking their peers, "Is he really the professor?" Initially, I used to think that they asked me this question because of my age, or because I look younger than they may have expected. However, after I was asked the same question numerous times, I arrived at the conclusion that it cannot only be about my young-looking face and that there must be something else behind this curiosity and persistent astonishment.

Moreover, through social interaction with culturally, racially, and linguistically insensitive people, I am often reminded of my "foreign" status. Those who choose to be blunt usually say, "You speak with a foreign accent. Where is it from?" I always respond that I am from Haiti. However, the challenge is

BELONGING NEITHER HERE NOR THERE

that sometimes those who are curious to know where my accent originates have trouble geographically locating Haiti. They often ask if Haiti is located in Africa. Often I have to educate them about other parts of the world of which they are not aware.

Those who hastily assume I'm from Africa seem to base their assumption on my dark skin and other physical traits, such as my flat nose and big lips. I challenge them by pointing out that not all dark-skinned people with these physical characteristics are from Africa. I try to do so in a way that does not embarrass them or belittle their humanity, as I do not want to reproduce the same insensitive and oppressive practices of others. Paulo Freire (1993) in the *Pedagogy of the Oppressed* and Albert Memmi (1991) in *The Colonizer and the Colonized* argued that the formerly oppressed and colonized often tend to reproduce the same oppressive practices of which they were once victims. I refuse to do so.

Undeniably, having a discernable accent has added another layer to my identity. However, as a professor teaching courses on language, culture, literacy, and theories and methods about second-language acquisition, it is not speaking the hegemonic English language with a foreign accent that concerns me; rather, it is people's xenophobic, racist, and classist attitude toward that accent. Situating the accent issue in a cultural, sociopolitical, racial, and ideological context, I argue that one's accent most likely would not be a problem if one were a White European, especially from northern or western Europe. This phenomenon is clearly visible in today's culture. For example, the heavily accented California governor, Arnold Schwarzenegger, was once touted as a potential presidential candidate despite his ineligibility as an Austrian-born immigrant.

I contend that the accent issue needs to be linked to other issues, such as one's native tongue, social class, race, and country of origin, and the dominance of the English language. This dominance often results in the oppression of other languages. According to Macedo and his colleagues (2003), in the United States, languages other than the hegemonic English language have been attacked by conservative intellectuals such as Diane Ravitch (1990), E. D. Hirsch Jr. (1987), and Allan Bloom (1989), who have fiercely rejected multiculturalism and bilingualism and advocated for a "common culture" (Hirsch, 1987). Given the hegemonic domination of the English language, combined with xenophobic, racist, and classist attitudes, it is not surprising that many immigrants who speak with a "foreign accent" feel alienated. Personally, having been positioned as the "*other*" countless times due to my racial and linguistic backgrounds, and my country of origin, I, at times, feel like an unwanted individual in this country despite my naturalized American citizenship and, most importantly, my decades of contribution to its academic and socio-economic progress.

5 Conclusion

I do not feel protected under the same human and legal rights that White middle and upper class Americans particularly enjoy, complicating the whole notion of citizenship. Factors such as race, White privileges, and country of origin should challenge me to rethink and question the notion of citizenship, as these factors often determine who in this country is actually treated with dignity and inclusivity as a citizen, and who is not. In the case of those who renounce their nationality to become American citizens, the notion is even more problematic. Many of these immigrants, except perhaps those of western European descent, never feel treated as Americans because of their racial, linguistic, and cultural backgrounds, and countries of origin. Personally, like many African Americans, Native Americans, Latinx, and Asians, I am fully aware that regardless of my current status as a professor, I will always be treated as the "other" due to my racial background as well my accent and birth land. This is an unpleasant feeling that no one should experience, including those from the global South who have contributed to the socioeconomic and cultural growth of this country. Unfortunately, due to systemic racism, White supremacy, xenophobia, this sense of dislocation persists among Americans, born and non-born.

CHAPTER 5

To Be Non-White in America Is to Be in Danger

To be Black or Brown is to be in danger. I am fully cognizant of the fact that the word danger has negative connotation. This word has rarely been used to refer to anything positive. It has rather been utilized to refer to people who are violent, or are perceived as such, objects, or events that no one wants to deal with. Blacks are often seen as a danger even when they are themselves in danger. For example, Blacks are seen as a danger while seeking help on the street or any public facility, or simply walking.

Similarly, while laboring in sugarcane and cotton plantations to enrich the masters, our ancestors were seen as a danger. What is more, both enslaved and freed African Americans that were forced to leave the South for the North to escape being lynched and to seek employments were feared and seen as a danger. Finally, we have witnessed in modern history similar racial phenomenon with immigrants of color moving in masses to Europe and the United States seeking a better life; they are, too, seen as a danger.

Because of the challenges noted above, psychologically it feels, at times, like a burden being Black in White America where Blacks have been killed nearly every day. I am aware that associating the word burden with the experiences of Blacks makes matter worse given historically negative phrases or words, such as black market, blackmail, blacklist, and blackout, among many others, have been associated with the word black. Therefore, the reader might rightfully ask: Why do I use the word burden to refer to Blacks? Isn't disrespectful to the pioneers of the negritude and the Civil Rights movements and the Black Panthers party who sacrificed their lives for black liberation, including mental liberation, and have inspired billions of Blacks around the world to battle against systemic racism, imperialism, and colonialism, to dare associate the word burden to Blacks? To those who may be asking these questions, I feel that I owe them an explanation regarding the context in which I use the word burden in this book. To this end, I wish to begin with a story embedded in a family ritual, which has shaped my childhood, adolescence, and adulthood memories.

I am reminded when I was a boy, my mother used quite often the Creole word "fado," which means burden, while complaining about challenges she faced as a single mother raising four children. She often cried while reading her bible, singing, or praying at night. She would say, "Oh mon dye, sil vou ple, edem pote fado sa. Mwen pakap anko. Mwen fatige."[1] My mother would also call on her deceased mother whose spirit she trusted would protect her and give her the

© KONINKLIJKE BRILL NV, LEIDEN, 2020 | DOI: 10.1163/9789004440944_006

strength needed to continue her long journey on this earth as a single mother. She would pray every night before she went to bed and again at dawn before she started her long day as an entrepreneur.

As a boy who could not make sense of the content of my mother's nightly ritual, I often asked her why she was crying. She would respond, "I am okay my son," and she would then continue to cry while using the word burden. She never took the time to explain to me why she burst into tears while praying. Perhaps, she assumed that I was too young, so I would not understand what she was going through. Or perhaps she did not want to make me sad. My mother always tried to make her children happy by trying hard to provide for them. At times, I would also cry when I saw her crying. She would then stop crying and try to console me. But she never explained to me why she used the word burden while praying. This was a family ritual, which is deeply registered in my mind.

It has been more than 20 years since I left the island; I have not had a chance to be a part of this family ritual that I grew up with since I left. I have learned to appreciate it as I got older. This ritual has become part of my spiritual life in the sense that each time I am confronted with terrific personal and professional challenges in my life, I say a prayer silently asking invisible spiritual forces to help me remain strong and show me a way out of them. The word burden, as it is used in this book, emerges out of both family rituals and my daily experience as a Black man battling against individual and institutional racism in the United States. While my mother used the word burden to refer to her daily socioeconomic and emotional challenges she was facing as a single parent of four children, I am using it in this book to refer to, the ill treatment and racial aggression that Black and Brown people, including myself, have faced despite their professional achievements.

1   Perceived and Treated as a Problem in America

This book is deeply grounded in my personal, professional, and existential experiences as a Black man who has been facing both institutional racism and xenophobia in America, including in the White Ivory Tower, as a professor. My blackness, like anybody's blackness, is ill perceived and poorly treated in the Americas due to systemic racism and White supremacy.

It is not my blackness or anybody's blackness that is the burden. Rather, it is the daily struggle dealing with systemic racism, White supremacy, and xenophobia. For example, isn't a burden having to constantly worry about racial profiling, like being pulled over by police officers who choose to stop you merely because they assume you might have drugs or guns in your car, or being followed in stores because of your skin tone? Also, isn't a burden worrying one might receive death penalty for a crime you did not commit? When I started writing book, the controversial case of a Black man named Troy Davis made the headlines. According to popular opinion, Mr. Davis was unfairly executed after being accused of shooting a police officer in 1989. Some people argued Davis' case was nothing but a legalized lynching.

Alluding to Troy Davis' execution, isn't fair to say any Black man could have been a victim of social injustice like Davis had? Isn't a burden feeling that your life, like that of Davis as a Black man, can be taken away by a racially biased justice system? Isn't a burden to be afraid of being unfairly shot by police officers, like it was the case of Amadou Diallo, Sean Bell, and Oscar Grant – the three unarmed young Black men, among many others, who were murdered by police officers? Isn't a burden having to constantly prove your intelligence to people who have historically made you believe that genetically you're not smart? Isn't a burden having to constantly battle against symbolic violence? Isn't a burden just thinking that you can be denied employment and housing because of your skin tone? Finally, isn't a burden having to prove to people that you're smart because of their racist attitude and behavior?

Despite these words of caution that I utter, I am fully cognizant of the fact that my narrative, embedded in my racial, linguistic, socioeconomic, and political struggles, might be interpreted by some people as a book written by an angry Black man. Instead, I invite the reader to see my testiminio as the inconvenient truth from a Black man who is courageous to affirm his humanity in the face of inequities.

My goal is to share with people, especially those who do not know how, and possibly will never know how, it is like to be Black and be placed on the edge of the White world. My narratives in this book aim to showcase the psychological burden having to be concerned about blackness, as a result of the unbearable weight of overt and subtle forms of systemic racism that I have been facing. Despite many similarities existing among Blacks across the Atlantic, one's experience as a Black man remains fundamentally unique because of the various factors mentioned earlier. This is to say that my experience as a Black man from the Caribbean may not be the same as that of other Blackmen, including those who are from Africa and other parts of the word. My experience might also differ from the daily experience of African Americans, especially those who were born and grew up during the Jim Crow era and slavery.

2 Experiencing Inequities in the Main Land

Before becoming a multilingual case manager, a high school teacher, a university professor, and a father, I used to wash dishes and clean floors in nursing homes, malls, and in hotels, including five star hotels, like the Four Seasons Hotel located in Boston, Massachusetts. Working as a dishwasher and housekeeper at these places enabled me to understand what it was like to work two jobs and yet unable able to make ends meet. The six years I spent toiling at these places were the most painful and humbling experiences I could have ever had as a poor working class immigrant.

Even though I had college student status, I was ill-treated. We were all overworked and underpaid. Most of my coworkers were immigrants who had no opportunity to attend college neither here nor in their native lands. In fact, while some did not finish high school, others barely knew how to read and write but managed to secure and maintain jobs. Many of my immigrant co-workers did not have the luxury to go to school to improve their English skills because they had to work two jobs to support themselves and their families. Even though they had been living in the U.S. for more than a decade, they could barely speak English: They were too busy working two jobs to feed themselves and their families. Many immigrated to this country with their families to seek a better life.

Though we were doing the same menial and low-paying jobs, I was privileged in the sense that I knew these jobs were temporary and that as soon as I finished college, I would find a better job. By contrast, my coworkers did not seem to be as hopeful. Indeed, when I visited the places, including the hotel, where I used to work, I observed that many of my coworkers were doing the same jobs that I left. This experience confirmed what I have always believed: social class is fluid and it thus can be transcended.

One can move up from being poor or working class to being a university professor, for example, provided one has the opportunity to go to college and earn a degree, although having a college degree does not necessarily guarantee jobs or good jobs. For example, many people, particularly people of color, with PhDs are struggling to make ends meet. Race matters. My coworkers were people of color from various ethnic backgrounds and different places in the world, such as the Caribbean, Africa, and Latin America. I do not believe that was coincidental. My experience, along with the experiences of family and friends who have worked at blue-collar jobs, suggest to me that people of color, including immigrants of color, tend to be the ones who do, or are forced to do, low-paying jobs, like washing dishes and cleaning in restaurants and hotels. Poor Whites also do these types of jobs. The capitalist system exploits people regardless of their skin tone, although due to institutional racism, Blacks,

TO BE NON-WHITE IN AMERICA IS TO BE IN DANGER   57

Latino, Native American, and Asian workers are often treated worse than their poor White coworkers at the same job. As for female workers, the treatment they often receive from their bosses and male coworkers is often far worse than anybody else's, particularly female workers of color.

I witnessed similar inequity and unfairness teaching minority students in the most marginalized high school in Boston, Massachusetts. This experience has helped me better understand how racial inequality impacts the learning and academic growth of minority students. This high school was underfunded, so many caring and dedicated teachers had to teach their poor students of color and Whites under horrible working conditions. For example, school materials were scarce; consequently, many of my colleagues and I had to use our own money to buy school supplies. Worse yet, many of us were forced to leave our teaching jobs because of budget cuts. I was one of the teachers who were laid off years ago. I questioned and still question why schools in poor neighborhood serving poor children of color and poor Whites are always the first ones to drastically suffer from state and federal budget cuts. Shouldn't these schools be the least affected by these cuts?

Furthermore, as an instructor at both a community and a small liberal-arts college in Massachusetts, where I taught and worked with working-class people of color, including immigrant students of color, I continued to witness inequalities in school. Single mothers of color enrolled in my classes had to miss classes because they did not have transportation. In fact, many had to discontinue their schooling because of a lack of support and resources. Specifically, many had to get a second job in the midst of the semester to make ends meet; consequently, they dropped out of my classes.

These were committed and serious students of color whom I witnessed dropping out of college because of a lack of support and financial resources for single working mothers. I ask: Why doesn't the government allocate resources to create programs at colleges, especially community colleges where many of the students are among the working poor, to support single mothers so they can stay in school and finish college? Why does the government spend billions of dollars on wars and yet refuse to allocate adequate resources to educate poor working-class women? Should we talk about equity and social justice in a country where a tiny group of privileged people have most of the resources of the earth enabling them to attend elite colleges and universities and receive high-quality education while others do not even have the opportunity to finish an associate degree at a community college?

Meanwhile, corporate lies circulated in the mainstream media and schools want to make people believe they are living in a democratic society. As a product of a community college, where I earned my first college degree, I felt particularly touched by the racial, socio-economic conditions of my students. I could easily relate to many of them, for I had similar experiences as them. For example, while I was working on my associate degree at Massachusetts Bay Community College, I had to work two jobs in order to be able to pay my tuition, take care of myself, and support members of my family living in Haiti, whom I still help. Consequently, I slept and socialized much less, and was often broke while attending college.

Similarly, my experiences both as a former student and currently as faculty enabled me to witness racial injustice and inequity in institutions, such as the Ivy Tower. As a student, I personally witnessed and experienced racial disparity and inequality. I witnessed the difference between students of color and Caucasian students in terms of the unequal treatment they received from professors and peers. For example, I witnessed that some Caucasian classmates, particularly those who were complicit with the system, received better treatment from professors, particularly White professors, than did students of color. These White students had an easier time receiving graduate assistantships and had more opportunities to co-teach and publish with these professors than did graduate students of color, especially those who questioned the status quo.

The few students of color who had some privileges in terms of being allowed to co-teach and publish with some White professors were also complicit with the system. By taking classes and being involved for four years in a school-university partnership research project with them, I quickly realized they were very obedient and fearful of challenging their professors, especially those who were in charge of giving students assistantships. Yet, the empty talk about equity and diversity was taking place in some of the classes I was taking. These two notions, embedded in the U.S. Pledge of Allegiance, have also been a ritual in elementary, middle, and high schools. Students, teachers, and staff alike are expected to recite this allegiance like parrots.

The notion of equity, diversity, democracy, freedom, and social justice runs through departments and programs at universities. Ironically and sadly, even within departments and programs that claim to be democratic and to promote social justice and equity, one finds colleagues who are abusing their White, male, and senior status privileges. Many of these professors talk about democracy, social justice, and equity, yet during faculty meetings, in their classrooms, and in other contexts, they tend to silence, dominate, and psychologically wound, through their words and actions, junior faculty and students of color (Matsuda, Lawrence, Delgado, & Crenshaw, 1993).

These colleagues didn't realize that junior faculty, female students, and students of color were assessing their prejudiced behaviors and actions. Nor did they seem to realize that they were often abusing their male privileges, which allowed many of them to be in position of power. They lacked such awareness and yet they continued to label themselves as progressives and social-justice educators, including the self labeled White allies. Their daily actions and inter-actions with both junior faculty and students of color revealed something different, especially in the eyes of those whose voice they often tried to silence. These professors, failing to question their White privileges, which they acted upon, often treated students and colleagues of color as subaltern. My experi-ences as a Black facing multiple forms of oppression in the United have shaped my consciousness about inequalities while at the same time pushing me to succeed in my small ways.

Note

1   Oh God! Please help me carry this burden. I am no longer able to carry it. I am tired.

CHAPTER 6

Succeeding as Black in an Uneven Western World

In this chapter, I draw on my personal narrative as a form of inquiry to examine how certain labels have been racially, socially, culturally, and historically constructed and imposed on minorities living in the United States, and I am not an exception. The imposition of these labels on people often leads to people's marginalized position in society. As I would explain in detail later, because various labels have been placed on me, I am often perceived and treated as the "other" and my voice has consequently been silenced at times. Professors and colleagues at institutions, where I studied and have taught, have often performed and behaved as if they are the ones who have access to power and knowledge (Foucault, 1995), and many of them have used use master narratives to speak on my behalf, thereby misrepresenting me. It is therefore imperative that I, as someone of color from a poor working class background, intervene to counter these narratives and tell my authentic stories because, as Coloma (2008) argues, "The desire to speak for oneself is especially important for marginalized individuals and communities that have been imagined and represented by those who occupy dominant positions of power" (p. 11). Coloma adds, "For the marginalized, at stake is the right of self-definition and self-determination. The refusal to be silent is a necessary and vigilant act of affirmation and resistance" (p. 12). Building on Coloma's views, I argue that my-liberation from oppression cannot be achieved while remaining silent, whether due to self-censorship or pressure from by those in power. Therefore, exploring the possibility of articulating my own story is a great step toward my self-liberation.

1 Challenges

I have faced two major challenges since I have been living in the United States: (1) being a Black, particularly from a Third World country, and (2) speaking English in a non-native accent. I have had painful experiences resulting from these racial and linguistic markers. In Haiti, I was merely Haitian and treated as such. However, after I moved to the United States, my identity changed dramatically: I am not only Black but an immigrant, a minority, and a "boat person," as Haitian immigrants are so often portrayed in the mainstream media.

© KONINKLIJKE BRILL NV, LEIDEN, 2020 | DOI: 10.1163/9789004440944_007

SUCCEEDING AS BLACK IN AN UNEVEN WESTERN WORLD

These are social identities or labels that I did not construct myself. They have been arbitrarily imposed on me, and I have to deal with their repercussions.

I was never referred to as Black or, worse yet, called nigger, while living in my native land. Therefore, I never had to worry about my Blackness or bear the psychological wounds and pain that come along with it (Matsuda et al., 1993). However, for the past 25 years or more that I have been living in this country, I have been treated primarily as Black, regardless of my social class. I have been socially compelled to constantly worry about my Blackness. My Black skin has made me a target. By virtue of being Black, I have been discriminated against at school and in other settings. I have also been discriminated against because of my nonstandard way of speaking English. In the following section, I further explicate the way I have been linguistically discriminated against.

2   Confronting Linguistic and Racial Discrimination

I did not start speaking English until I was 24 years old. This is the reality of many immigrants. I vividly remember the challenges that I faced learning a new language and adjusting to a new culture. It helped tremendously that I already spoke two languages before immigrating to the U.S., for I was able to transfer the knowledge acquired in my native tongue, Haitian Creole, and my first academic language, French, to the target language, English. However, these linguistic assets did not save me from the cultural shock that I encountered here in the U.S; nor did they protect me from xenophobia, linguistic, and racial discrimination that I experienced in college. I am reminded of a horrible experience that I had presenting a paper in one of my undergraduate classes.

With my limited English speaking skills, I was required to share with my monolingual classmates and the instructor my final paper by doing a presentation in class. After I finished presenting the paper, the instructor asked my classmates if they had any questions for me. Several students asked me questions, to which I responded. Then a White female student named Jennifer, who was sitting next to me, shouted, "I didn't understand anything he was saying; how can I then ask him any question?" There was a silence in the class after Jennifer made this comment. The instructor, who pretended that nothing happened, proceeded to ask if any student had any questions for me.

I stood frozen and felt ashamed in front of the whole class after Jennifer made this insensitive comment. What I found particularly shocking about her comment was the fact that everyone else did not seem to have a problem understanding me but her. Furthermore, I was suspicious of Jennifer's comment because, since the beginning of the semester, she showed a lack of tolerance and respect toward me when I spoke in class. For example, she interrupted me several times while talking as if the questions I was asking or comments I was making in class were not important, or annoyed her.

I went home that day thinking about dropping out of the class. I even thought about dropping out of college, fearing that I would not be able to complete my associate degree at the community college that I was attending due to my temporary English-language barrier. When I returned to class the following week, I was hoping that Jennifer would apologize to me for humiliating me in front of everyone in that class, but she never did. For the remainder of that semester, I became tongue tied and remained silent. I stopped talking in class, fearing my classmates, especially Jennifer, would look down on me for not being able to speak like they did.

This painful experience has caused a linguistic inferiority complex in the English language. That is, even though I am now fluent and proficient in English, I still question my oral competency and ability in English. I still experience some level of inner fear when I speak English, especially in front of people I barely know. I feel this inner fear much more strongly when talking to a native speaker and he/she says to me, "What did you say?" or "Can you repeat what you said because I didn't understand you." Or, worse yet, when people say to me, "You're a professor, really? In what language do you teach? Is it in French?" I have gotten this xenophobic reaction even from people for whom English is their second or third language and whose accent is much heavier than mine.

It seems to me that uninformed people tend to equate having a "foreign" accent with a lack of intelligence. In other words, if one does not speak like an "American," that is, like a middle-class White American, one's intelligence has to be questioned, and one's native language, if not English, can't be appreciated and respected. In my view, this type of attitude has helped the proponents of the English-only movement to attack and eliminate bilingual programs in states such as California, Arizona, and Massachusetts. This attitude has also helped create a stronger climate of xenophobia in the United States.

While I was finishing my associate degree at that community college, I had another painful experience with an English professor named Mathis. I took an English composition class with him after my sister-in-law assured me that I would do well in his class. She trusted that I would do well based on the fact that I helped my older brother with his English assignments when he was taking the same class but with a different professor. Though I was not orally proficient in the English language, I was able to read and write it fairly well. Furthermore, having already acquired academic discourse in my second language, French, I was able to write in an academic fashion in English though with some difficulties.

SUCCEEDING AS BLACK IN AN UNEVEN WESTERN WORLD

However, despite my strong academic background prior to joining Professor Mathis's class, I had an awful experience taking this English composition class with him. He scorned me numerous times for not being able to speak English well. He questioned whether I was the one who did my assignments for his class. He questioned my intelligence. Apparently, he equated my lack of fluency in the English language to lower intelligence. While he encouraged my classmates to meet with him during his office hours, he would not do the same for me.

I could not stop thinking that Professor Mathis was xenophobic and racist and that he did not want to waste his time meeting with someone who does not look like and speak like him. In his class, I was the only Black person and the only student for whom English was not his first language. Being determined to not give up and drop his class, I took the initiative to ask him for an appointment. He pressured me to explain to him why I wanted to meet with him – I doubt he asked the same of my classmates when they made an appointment. Professor Mathis made me feel like I was a lost case, undeserving of his time and attention.

When we met, I explained to him that I was formally educated in my native land and that I was only experiencing a temporary language barrier. After the meeting, I noticed he started showing some level of human compassion toward me. He suggested that instead of taking the required final test, I could prepare a portfolio as the final project of his class, which would allow me to take English 102. He said he doubted I would pass that test. Being resolute to prove him wrong, I studied as hard as possible and took the test, which I passed. After I passed that test, moved to English 102, and graduated from the community college, I did not see Professor Mathis until 11 years later on the campus of University of Massachusetts at Amherst, where I was pursuing a doctorate degree.

I unexpected ran into Professor Mathis when he was visiting that university. "Are you Professor Mathis?" I asked.

"Yes, I am," he said. "You're Pierre, right? Weren't you in my English class at Massachusetts Bay Community College,?"

I said, yes, I was.

He asked what I was doing at the university.

"I am finishing a doctorate in education," I said.

In a surprised tone, he replied, "Oh, wow! Really? Good for you!"

I thanked him and asked what he was doing here. Reluctantly, he said, "I am considering applying for the doctoral program in the English Department here." We talked for a while and wished each other good luck as we said good-bye.

My racist and xenophobic experiences show that we have a long way to go before we can honestly and genuinely talk about democracy and social justice for all in this country. My painful experiences with my classmate Jennifer and Professor Mathis inspired me to pursue a master's degree in Applied Linguistics with a concentration in ESL (English as a second language), aiming to help immigrant children acquire English and critical thinking skills. While I was working on my master's degree and later on my doctoral degree, I had the privilege to be acquainted with, mentored by, take classes from, and work with phenomenal scholars such as Sonia Nieto and Donaldo Macedo, who are deeply vested in multicultural and bilingual education issues. These scholars inspired me to further explore these issues beyond the walls of the classroom. Ever since my graduate work, I have been exploring the history and politics of language in the U.S. and beyond. The knowledge that I have acquired exploring the literature on language issues helped me understand the underlying reasons that may have led many people to discriminate against those who speak hegemonic languages like English and French with a foreign accent.

Specifically, I have learned that language is not neutral. It is intrinsically linked to ideology and unequal power relations between dominant and subjugated languages. Historically, those in power have always attempted to force those in subordinate positions in society to speak and embrace their dominant culture and language. As Ngũgĩ Wa Thiong'o eloquently pointed out in his book *Decolonising the Mind,* this form of oppression can be traced back to the colonial period where the colonizers forced the colonized to speak their dominant languages (Thiong'o, 1986). This form of linguistic oppression has been revived in the so-called modern or postmodern time through western neocolonial-language domestic and foreign policies such the English-only movement in the U.S. (Macedo, Dendrinos, & Gounari, 2003).

In the United States, for example, forcing minoritized people to speak English at the expense of their native languages is, in my view, a neocolonial form of linguistic domination. Invading and occupying countries and expecting the people in the occupied lands to speak the invaders' and occupiers' language and embrace their western lifestyle is a renewed form of colonialism disguised with a different mask (Pennycook, 1996, 2003). Finally, preventing minoritized students from speaking and embracing their own language(s) for fear they would not be fully integrated in the dominant culture is a way of colonizing their mind and soul (Thiong'o, 1986). In my view, there is no other name for this form of domination but "linguistic imperialism" (Phillipson, 1992).

Racial and linguistic discrimination is a daily reality for many people of color, including myself, as they continue both their professional and academic journey here in the U.S. In the section that follows, I use my experience teaching and working with immigrant students to further illustrate racial and linguistic marginalization to which minority students of color have been subjected.

SUCCEEDING AS BLACK IN AN UNEVEN WESTERN WORLD

3 Lessons Learned from My Personal Journey

In my experience both as a student and a professor, I have learned that highly dedicated students and professors of color are discriminated against because of their racial and linguistic backgrounds and their nationality. For example, I have always had to prove my intelligence and intellectual ability to people, especially because I refuse to be unfairly and incorrectly labeled as the beneficiary of affirmative action, though many are aware that White women have benefited more from this law than have people of color. Challenging this prejudicial assumption about minorities, Carlos Munoz (Schneider, 1998), a university professor of color stated, "Minority job applicants must be superstars to be able to say that 'now you can't deny that I am qualified'" (p. 11).

Of course, I'm not the only one being targeted because of my racial background. Other professors of color have also been victims of individual and institutional racism. For example, the distinguished U.S. legal scholar Richard Delgado has faced racial invisibility with some of his White colleagues. According to Delgado: "Many of my White colleagues do not really know what a Latino is. Others know, but barely tolerate me, even though I am one of the top legal publishers in the country and well liked by my students" (Delgado, xxx, as cited in Orelus, 2011, p. 11).

Likewise, Sharon Subreenduth (2008), a South African professor of color teaching at Bowling Green State University, faced similar xenophobic and racial discriminations in the U.S. academy. In a narrative essay, "Deconstructing the Politics of a Differently Colored Transnational Identity," Subreenduth described how a White American senior researcher dismissed and stripped her of her South African identity and her commitments to conduct research in her native land, South Africa. The White senior researcher had done some research in South Africa and represented himself as an expert in South Africa's history, culture, and politics while misrepresenting Subbreenduth, a junior faculty, as the "other." Not surprisingly, Subreenduth was unhappy with the way the White senior researcher treated her. Drawing on her painful experience with the White American researcher, Subreenduth (2008) suggested that, "In order to rupture the underpinnings of oppression, one needs to counter and disrupt the operation of othering and objectification within academia and academic spaces" (p. 43).

Certainly, the examples given above are only a few among many. Countless similar examples can be given here to further illustrate how those in powerful positions in the U.S. academy often use the racial, ethnic, and linguistic backgrounds of professors of color to marginalize them, and how such treatment has negatively impacted their identities and material conditions. The key point that needs to be emphasized is that one cannot and should not detach one form of oppression from another, for all forms of oppression are interconnected. In other words, racism, linguicism, and xenophobia, among others, are interrelated and therefore should not be analyzed separately; they all need to be part of the larger discussion and analysis of social injustice facing people of color in the West and beyond.

While my narrative reflects first and foremost my long personal and professional struggles to affirm my multiple identities in a so-called U.S. democratic land, it also reflects the stories shared by many people of color. As Lee Anne Bell (2010) puts it, "As we link our individual stories into a collective story we discern patterns of racism. We see how dominance and subordination are engendered, even against our desires. We witness how or stories are interconnected, how advantage and disadvantage are constructed" (p. 51). I argue that stories like mine as well as those of other oppressed groups need to continue to be told as counternarratives to grand narratives, which mainly reflect the voice of dominant groups. The authentic voice of those who have been marginalized can be genuinely heard through their own narratives, but not through truncated versions of such narratives as reported in western history textbooks.

The narratives of oppressed people that have been relegated to the periphery for decades must be rewritten to challenge those in position of power who have often labeled it as being "story telling" or "too emotional." This dominant discourse only serves to perpetuate the primacy of western grand narratives permeating most canonical texts. Counter narratives are used as a form of inquiry to articulate one's story with one's voice is a great step toward self-liberation; one's liberation lies in one's dissident voice. In the following chapter, I expand on my experiences teaching in predominantly White institutions, namely the U.S. academy.

CHAPTER 7

What It Means Being Black in the Ivy Halls of White America

While growing up in Haiti, facing grinding poverty was my daily reality. In my surroundings, I could not have ever missed it because of the multiple ghettoized neighborhoods where I lived. More pointedly, and perhaps worse, the number of accumulated piles of garbage on almost every corner of the neighborhood where I lived, the amount of noise that frequently prevented me from concentrating on my homework and sleeping well at night, the amount of crowded poor people living next to me, and the number of starving looking children running on the street barefooted reminded me constantly that I was indeed poor because rich people do not live in such environment.

Although I have continued to witness poverty in the United States, I am no longer poor. Race has been by far of more an issue for me than class. This is not to suggest that racial issues are more important than ones; all forms of oppression are connected and hurt. When I first immigrated to this country, both race and class were my major concerns as a poor working class immigrant of color. As a dishwasher and housekeeper who had to work two jobs to make basic ends meet and who had been racially discriminated against on countless occasions and at many places (at stores, on the street, in schools, hotels, airports, etc), I could not close my eyes on classism and racism. Furthermore, worrying constantly about how I was going to be able to pay my monthly bills, including my school tuition, made me realize that class matters. Finally, my experience as a graduate student selling my labor as an adjunct professor teaching courses here and there at various institutions so I could meet my basic needs made me realize that social class is serious issue. Graduate students from wealthy families do not have to do what I did for several years as a graduate student of color.

Now, as a university professor with a much higher salary, my wife and I, at times, have to juggle between wants and needs. This is not to suggest that I am denying my class privileges, which have enabled me to have access to cultural, social, and symbolic capital. I am fully aware that because of my social status, I have a higher chance being taken seriously and trusted than a poor Black person with a high school diploma or a lesser degree. I am also aware that I will have a higher chance than a poor Black person to be granted credit, for example, to buy a car or a house because of my social class. Finally, because

© KONINKLIJKE BRILL NV, LEIDEN, 2020 | DOI: 10.1163/9789004440944_008

of classism, I am cognizant of the fact that, unfortunately, society in general would think higher of me and show me more respect than someone without a college degree.

Nonetheless, despite these class privileges, I am and will always be seen and treated as a Black man when, for example, I am driving, walking on the street, shopping at a store, teaching, leading faculty meetings as department chair, attending committee meetings, presenting at professional conferences, interacting with colleagues, giving talks at universities and colleges, going through airport security, dinning at a restaurant, and playing with my kids at the park, or taking a walk in my neighborhood. In other words, my race has subsumed and will continue to subsume my social class status as a university professor in this racist society. My social class has not and will never protect me from racial profiling that I have experienced at stores or while driving. Nor has it saved me from being seen and at times used as a token to fake racial diversity on college campuses and universities. Finally, my social class status as a university professor has not and will not salvage me from constant suspicion my neighbors have shown towards me.

For instance, I am currently living in a neighborhood inhabited mostly by White and upper middle class people. Even though my family and I have been living there for three years, I still feel like a stranger. Despite my effort to reach to some of my neighbors, I have not been able to connect with many of them. On many occasions, some have even turned their face away from me while I was trying to greet them, whereas others would just walk by me without greeting me. However, it is hoped that someday these neighbors will see me beyond my skin tone and try to engage me as a person.

While I will never take for granted my social class status as a university professor and administrator, I am not naïve to believe that people see first and foremost my social class when I am walking on the university campus. In other words, when I am walking on the university campus, I am simply a visible Black man, although at times I can be invisible depending on the context, like Ralph Ellison (1980) eloquently described in his book *Invisible Man*. For example, I was sitting at a table talking to a colleague who happened to be a White male. A high rank person at my university came in; she completely ignored me, and went directly to my colleague and talked to him. This person behaved as if she never met me before and that I was not at the table, even though I was sitting right next to my colleague and it was only the two of us who were sitting at the table. After this incident occurred, many questions crossed my mind, such as: Did this person ignore me because I am Black? Or did this person do so because I am a professor over whom she has power? Or did this person have an issue with my ideological position? Or was this person simply being plain rude?

WHAT IT MEANS BEING BLACK IN THE IVY HALLS OF WHITE AMERICA

I went home that day asking my wife whether she thought I should be looking for a tenure track position elsewhere, as I felt unsafe after I experienced this form of racial invisibility. This high rank person will be one of the people deciding whether I should be granted promotion or not. Despite my fear and sense of uncertainty, I decided that I would stay at the institution with the hope that my credentials will enable me get promotion. My plan is that if they deny me promotion as a result of institutional racism and bigotry, I will legally challenge such a decision, as I feel that I already met promotion requirements. In fact, in the words of some senior professors, who reviewed my performance evaluation every year, I already met the expectations set for tenure and promotion as far as my scholarship was concerned.

At my past institution, when I was not invisible in the eyes of some high rank individuals and some racially prejudiced students, I was mistaken for a custodian. As a Black man, that's the social class status and label, informed by racial prejudice, often associated with me. In some people's prejudiced thinking, I could not possibly be a professor. In other words, my status as professor is not what crosses people's mind on college campuses when they see me. The questions that I have often gotten from people on and off campus are the following: Are you in the military? Are you playing football or basketball for the university, even though I am not the stereotypical tall or big man one would assume being involved in such sport? I feel exhausted having to explain to people that I have never been a soldier and that I am not a football or basketball player. In other words, I am exhausted having to correct, educate, and call people on their ignorant, racist questions and comments about my ethnic identity.

Sadly, I must acknowledge that people's assumption about me as a Black man is not too far off from the historical truth about the struggles of Black people in general. Historically, only a few people of African descent have been given the opportunity to earn advanced college degrees, like a doctorate, which would enable them to hold key and prestigious positions at universities. Even those with PhDs often face obstacles to secure a permanent professorship position at universities or high positions at other institutions, despite the empty rhetoric about diversity and equity running through university campuses. The reality on college and university campuses in terms of racial integration and equal opportunities to have access to well-paid positions suggests that we as a society have a long way to go before we can honestly talk about a fair representation of people of all races and ethnicities at these institutions.

Ironically at these institutions, the word diversity has been used as a commodity in their website to attract students and faculty of color and other underrepresented groups. Specifically, many institutions have used a few images of tokenized Black and Brown people in their websites to mislead people into believing that these institutions are racially diverse. The few faculty and students of color these institutions selectively recruit often do not receive the support they need to succeed. Many eventually leave. To my knowledge, the few who choose to stay are usually isolated and unhappy, and often fail. When they fail, the institutions often blame them for their failure, refusing to admit they have actually failed them by not giving them the support they need to succeed. I witnessed and personally experienced this deceiving and dishonest action as both an undergraduate and graduate student, and I have continued to undergo so as a professor.

Historically, privileged Christian, able-bodied, and heterosexual White males have been for the most part the ones running institutions, such as universities and colleges (Blumenfeld, 2006; Jensen, 2004; McIntosh, 1992; Lynn, Riser, & Yeigh, 2018). They are the ones who predominantly hold key positions ranging from being presidents, chancellors, provosts, vice provosts to being deans, associate deans, department chairs, and directors. Needless to say, they have the highest salary and have been in position to make decisions as to who should be hired as faculty, and who should be granted tenure and promotion, or full professorship. When professors of color, myself included, seeking assistant, associate, or full professorship positions at universities, they usually find themselves at the mercy of these privileged White males. We need a paradigmatic shift in the hierarchy that has shaped the western academy.

1 Longing for a Paradigm Shift: Will That Ever Occur?

For me personally, nothing has fundamentally changed as far as my racial condition is concerned. When I worked as a dishwasher and housekeeper at hotels, nursing homes, and malls I experienced racism. As both an undergraduate and graduate student, I also experienced racial harassment from police officers and clerks at stores. Now, as a university professor, I have continued to experience racial discrimination, stigmatization, and invisibility. The conclusion that I have drawn from these experiences is that it does not matter if my social status has changed from being a dishwasher, a housekeeper, a bilingual caseworker, a high school teacher, a doctoral student, to being a university professor. My blackness is a racial marker that has made me become a target, regardless of my status as a university professor. Because of my blackness, I do not feel safe, not even in classrooms where I have been teaching and preparing future teachers, educators, politicians, and lawyers.

To simply put it, my social class status as a university professor does not mean much as far as facing racism is concerned. Like any ordinary Black

WHAT IT MEANS BEING BLACK IN THE IVY HALLS OF WHITE AMERICA   71

person, I am subject to individual and institutional racism. By saying so, I do not mean that I should receive a different or a better treatment than poor and less educated Black people because of my social status as a university professor. Rather, what I intend to say is that in a racist society Blacks are not automatically protected because they move from being poor, working class people doing menial types of jobs at various places, to being university professors. This argument is in line with the racial profiling that the highly respected critical race theorist and legal scholar, Richard Delgado, experienced. It is worth citing him here. Delgado (2011) stated:

> Even dignified, well-dressed professionals encounter police profiling and challenges at work. I've been stopped by university police merely for looking out of place in the law building during evening hours. The incident had nothing to do with my income or class, but with my color and race. On other occasions, highway police have pulled me over just to check me out, even though I was driving a sober-looking rental car sedately and on my way back from an academic conference. (as cited in Orelus, 2011, p. 12)

Like Delgado, when I am driving to go to teach or to attend a conference, I am just a Black man in the eyes of the racist police officer. My blackness is what the officer sees first, and he or she will base on this racial marker to give me a citation. My social class status comes after my race. Likewise, when I am waiting for my wife on the corner of a street or on the sidewalk to come to pick me up, it is my blackness that makes some police officers suspicious of me assuming that I might be doing something illegal, like selling drugs. It is also my blackness that has made many police officers follow me when I am driving as a Black professor. In short, because of my blackness, I am always a suspect in the eye of police officers and many prejudiced individuals who hold deep prejudice about Blacks. My social status as a university professor does not matter much, if matters at all. What happened to prominent African American scholar, Cornel West, is a case in point. While driving in a 'White neighborhood,' Cornel West (1993) was pulled by a police officer, who accused him of drug trafficking. West stated:

> Years ago, while driving from New York to teach at Williams College, I was stopped on fake charges of trafficking cocaine. When I told the police officer I was a professor of religion, he replied, 'Yeah, and I'm the Flying Nun. Let's go, nigger!' I was stopped three times in my first ten days in Princeton for driving too slowly on a residential street with a speed limit of twenty-five miles per hour. (p. x)

Likewise, what Professor Antwi Akom experienced on university campus is a prime example of racial stigmatization of male professors of color. Noguera stated, "My friend and colleague Antwi Akom, a professor at San Francisco State University, was beaten and arrested by campus police when he entered his office at night (with his key) to retrieve a book while his two young daughters waited for him in their car" (p. xiv). I had the opportunity to interact with Professor Akom when he came to my past institution to talk about the intersection of race, class, the environment, health, and education. He talked about his unjustified arrest, and I could not help being angry listening to his story. I found Professor Akom to be a kind, friendly, and an intellectually sophisticated person. But these qualities do not matter in the eyes of the police officers whose racial prejudice led them to racially profile, arrest, and jail him. In their eyes, Professor Akom is just a Black man.

These examples are a few among many, for there are countless Black professors, students, and ordinary Black men and women who had experienced similar, if not worse, form of racial profiling that we might not be aware of. Nonetheless, Professors Delgado's, West's, Akom's, and my experiences with racial profiling clearly illuminate the point that I am trying to make about race. That is, a Black person is a Black person regardless of his or her social class, though a middle or upper class person can use his or her social class privileges to fight more effectively the racist legal system. For example, in some cases, one's social class can save one from going to or dying in jail, like in the high racially profiled case of O J Simpson in 1994. Had Mr. Simpson been a poor Black man, most likely he would have ended up in jail and possibly received death penalty years later. He was able to win the case because of his fame and money. However, his case is one of the few rare cases of Black men escaping the racially biased U.S. legal system.

The racial maker that is placed on Black people is done across the class and gender line. For example, a White professor is rarely, if ever, labeled a "White professor." However, a professor, like myself, who happens to be Black, is usually called "the Black professor." On many occasions, I have had students who approached me and asked: do you happen to know the male Black professor in the College of Education? They assumed that I knew who is that Black professor because I am Black myself. That Black professor happened to be me.

However, I never had any student, not even once, ask me this question when they were looking for a White professor. When I asked them for the Black professor's name, sometimes they knew it and sometimes they did not. People, including students, often use the racial identity of people of African descent to refer to them, but not their name assuming that those whom they ask about this or that Black professor should know who they are referring to.

WHAT IT MEANS BEING BLACK IN THE IVY HALLS OF WHITE AMERICA

There are not many Black professors at my current institution, let alone in my department. In my department, there are two Black professors: one who is the associate dean of the college and myself who has been serving as department chair. It was similar experience where I taught before. There were only two Black faculty members when I first joined the previous institution: An African American man who was dean. He was forced to step down as dean within a year but he remained as faculty as part of a legal settlement. I was told that his forcible resignation had much to do with institutional racism manifested through racial conspiracy against him.

Hence, despite the negative racial connotation associated with the types of questions students asked me when they were looking for a Black professor, it is understandable they assumed it will be easier to locate one by simply using a racial marker. Black professors and other professors of color are minorities on college and university campuses, with the exception of historically Black colleges and universities. Being either the only Black or one the few Black professors on college and university campuses is not rare, unfortunately. Because of a lack of a fair representation of faculty and administrators of color, (1) I am often asked to serve on committees just for the sake of having a Black face there; (2) I often feel overwhelmed having to serve as mentor or advisor to students of color who sometimes feel they can relate to you more than other colleagues; (3) whenever a racial or racist incident occurs, I am often called on to give my opinion about it; (4) I am usually seen as the expert on matters related to race, although I might not have been one; (5) I am often invited to give a talk during Black history month; (6) my name and/or picture is often used by the institution to promote their own definition of diversity; (7) I constantly feel the pressure to "keep it together" so my actions would not have bad repercussions on future people of color, especially Blacks; (8) because I am the only one or one of the few Black professors, I often get invited or asked to participate in many activities taking place on campus so that my "race" is represented; and (9) finally, directly or indirectly I am often expected to educate Whites about myself, my history, and the historical struggles of people of African descent in general.

If one day I am labeled a non-conformist or a radical Black professor, I probably, if ever, will not get invited to the things mentioned above. I anticipate this might happen possibly after the release of this book. The other Black or Brown professors who are "nice," meaning obedient, who do not question the status quo, would most likely receive all the attention or invitations to represent their race at the institutions where they work. These types of "nice" Black or Brown professors or administrators often get promoted to key positions to maintain the order of things for the benefits of those who control and rule universities or colleges. Whether they are aware of it or not, they contribute to maintaining institutional racism, for their presence is used strategically to cover up this form of racism. In other words, their mere presence might make the public believe that this or that university or college is racially diverse, even though the people who continue to run and attend it are predominantly Whites.

The pressure that Black professors, including myself, are under to "keep it together" often has negative consequences on their professional and personal lives and that of their families as a consequence. It is often assumed that somebody like myself will fail. In fact, I am expected to fail, and my failure would be used as an alibi to stigmatize other Blacks. For example, if I fail, my failure might be used to deny other Black professors the opportunity that I have had as a professor. The common racist argument that those in powerful positions at universities, colleges or other institutions often use to deny professional opportunities to Blacks is that they can't find qualified Black or Brown people for this or that position. What those who run and control these institutions have failed to realize or have refused to admit is that they have failed to support faculty of color by not providing them the support that they need, so that they can succeed. How can a predominantly White university expect dynamic and competent young Black or Brown professors to stay and succeed if they do not receive sufficient support and are provided with resources like solid mentorship from senior faculty, whose the majority are usually conservative Whites, who sometimes refuse to associate themselves with Black or Brown professors, let alone mentor them.

Nonetheless, the pressure to succeed, despite a lack of adequate support, is always hanging on the head on Black professors, like myself. Such pressure has compelled me to labor to a point where there is insufficient quality time left to spend with my family and loved ones, not to mention that my health has been affected as a result. For instance, during my first three years as a tenure track faculty of color I got sick more often than I had ever gotten sick before I became a professor. When I was not sick, I gained much weight as a result of many hours I spent sitting in front of my computer to write, so that I could keep up with the pressure of being 'productive.' Likewise, when I became department chair, I have undergone a high level of stress as I have been trying to prove myself. I have felt that I have to exceed institutional expectations in order to avoid being seen as the beneficiary of affirmative action. Specifically, I have felt the intense pressure to be as productive as I humanly can, so that some of my White students and colleagues, including self-proclaimed White allies, do not find any excuse to say that I am at my institution because I am Black. Because of White privilege supported by institutional racism, a White professor might not be harshly criticized for not being productive, but a professor of color like myself will inevitably be under the White gaze if I do not meet or exceed institutional expectations. This is the professional burden, among many others, that I have been forced to carry as a Black professor.

As far as I am concerned, the price for professional success has been heavy. My wife was pregnant when I moved from Easthampton, Massachusetts, to Las Cruces, New Mexico to take on a tenure track position right after I completed my doctorate. Being taken by the pressure to maintain a strong record of publication, teaching evaluation, to serve on many communities, and to present at conference almost destroyed the foundation of my marriage. By allowing myself to be absorbed by the academic world, I somewhat neglected my wife and my new-born baby. The sad part of all of this is that I was unaware this was happening until my wife started to protest and demanded that I helped in the house taking better care of my daughter and spending quality time with both of them.

The immense pressure that I have been facing as a faculty of color sometimes prevents me from spending quality time with my family. There was time when the pressure of meeting the requirements for promotion took my mind away while I should be playing with my children or giving my wife attention. I often had to make a conscious effort to remind myself that my undivided attention to my family is more important than anything else when I am home. Institutions have no memory. Therefore, no matter how much I do to feed the institutional machine, I will be forgotten when I leave. But not my family, if I take excellent care of them, they will always remember me beyond my death, let alone they will most likely take care of me when I am old.

Despite the fact that I am hard-pressed to keep up with my scholarship, teaching, and service, I have been trying the best I can to spend quality time with my family, including playing in the park or at home with my children. However, I am not always successful at doing so. My wife has mostly taken care of the kids, particularly my daughter. My experience being a father has made question my male privileges and my rhetoric about gender equality. Despite my willingness and conscious effort to be as fair as possible, I am not always successful. Sometimes, I feel somewhat guilty when I see my wife taking care of things in the house, including our kids, while I am trying to revise a manuscript for resubmission after it was rejected.

2   Teaching While Black: Confronting Whiteness in the Classroom

As a Black professor, I have to succeed not only in terms of research and service but also in terms of teaching. As far as teaching is concerned, I have some White students who seem to have a hard time accepting the fact I am their professor. For example, I had two White students who complained about my teaching style, whereas the majority of the students, who happen to be students of color, showed great appreciation for it. The most unpleasant experience that I had teaching was with two Caucasian students: one is Australian and the other an American.

This Australian student took two classes with me and one of which was a seminar. For these classes, I used as required texts two of Paulo Freire's books, *Pedagogy of the Oppressed* and T*eachers as Cultural Workers*, and *Turning to Learning* written By Carl Grant and Christine Sleeter. As a disclaimer, since I started teaching, I have been using Freire's pedagogical framework and philosophical approach of teaching to guide mine. I have urged students, especially pre-service teachers, not to take anyone's ideas and literally apply them in their classrooms upon becoming teachers. I have warned them, for example, saying that applying Freire's ideas inappropriately in a context which they do not understand would be a great disservice to themselves, their students, and that such an action might lead to the distortion of Freire's ideas. Moreover, I have reminded students that Freire encourages all educators to make a real effort to be fully aware of the context in which they teach because context matters. Finally, I have shared with them that Freire has also challenged educators to try to begin anew, opening their mind to new and fresh ideas. As Freire (1993) states, "This capacity to always begin anew, to make, to reconstruct, and to not spoil, to refuse to bureaucratize the mind, to understand and to live as a process – live to become – is something that always accompanied me throughout life. This is an indispensable quality of a good teacher" (p. 98).

However, these cautionary words and advice provided to students did not prevent me from encountering resistance from students in the classes aforementioned. For example, the Australian student mentioned earlier was finishing her Master's in TESOL (Teaching English to Speakers of Other Languages) when she took two classes with me. She fiercely resisted Freire's *Pedagogy of the Oppressed* assigned for a seminar class. She said this book was irrelevant to the focus of the class. When I tried to challenge her with the hope that she would look at teaching and education from a critically broader perspective, she became somewhat defensive and disregarded what some of her classmates and I had to say in class about Paulo Freire's philosophy of education. Worse, she even went to the dean of the college to complain about me, arguing she was not learning anything useful from my class.

For this seminar practicum class and other classes that I taught, students were required to post a weekly critique of the assigned readings on blackboard for their classmates to comment on. In a her reaction paper to the fourth chapter in Paulo Freire's book *Pedagogy of the Oppressed*, this particular student stated she found many hypocrisies in the chapter to a point that she felt like throwing up. She stated that she disagreed with the content of the chapter she read, stating that nobody could make a racial group think one way or another. She went further to say if we eliminate classism by getting rid of class, this would lead to the creation of a society that is not effective, that is, a society where people will not have any incentive to work hard in order to achieve. She concluded that, "The section on class was absolutely ridiculous. It is not okay to stereotype those considered of a lower class so why is it ok to stereotype those labeled in an upper class? The idea that people in an upper class want to keep others down is ridiculous. Why would one type of people wish harm on others just because they are affluent?" Finally, although I never engaged students in any discussion about President Barack Obama, this student wrote in her critique that she was very upset that some professors in the department wanted her to swallow the liberal ideas of President Obama.

My graduate assistant, who first read the student's critique, informed me about it immediately because, like me, he felt that there was much anger and bitterness in her critique. I decided to invite the student to come into my office to meet with me in order to discuss what might have prompted her heated reaction about the assigned chapter as well as her decision to complain to the dean of the college about my teaching practices. As she was talking, she was very apologetic and burst into tears. She could not give me a convincing reason for reacting the way she reacted about the assigned chapter, her defensive attitude and reaction toward my class, and her decision to tacitly report me to the dean. When I asked her why she did not bring up to my attention her concerns about the class before she decided to complain to the dean about it, she stated that she was dissatisfied with the whole program, which she felt only offered her theory but nothing practical she would be able to use to teach ESL, particularly grammar, to adult students. I challenged her reminding her that my class was not about teaching students how to teach grammar and that she should have read the class's description and goals before she took it.

Because I was shocked by this student's aggressive reaction about my class, I decided to talk to a senior faculty about the situation. He stated that her decision to report me to the dean could have been racially motivated, an opinion my graduate assistant and other colleagues shared. Although I suspected this might have been the case, I did not have any tangible evidence to support such an argument. The following semester, the same student took another course with me, for I was the only one who has been teaching such a course and she needed to take it so she could complete her Master's. I did not notice much change about her in terms of how she engaged the assigned reading and her classmates in class. Until she completed her Master's and left the program, I felt that she still held very different views of teaching and learning – she was seeking recipe from me, which she had hoped would enable her to teach grammar to ESL (English as a Second Language) students. Because I was not willing to feed her with prepackaged teaching recipe, she left my classes and, for that matter, the Bilingual and TESOL program very disappointed.

Why am I alluding here to this story? I am doing so to point out that we, as critical educators, have much more work to do to help students trapped in the banking form of education, which Paulo Freire brilliantly dissected and challenged us to reject, to develop and embrace instead a humanistic and transformative form of education. The banking form of education is obsolete and constitutes the antithesis of a liberatory form of education. That is, a form of education that has inspired and enabled many people, including students and teachers, to move from an object to a subject position in society.

The worst experience was with the White American student, who was not only disrespectful to me but also to some his female students of color and a Mexican-American woman instructor that I invited to speak in my class. In a graduate level course that I thought, there were twelve students; two of them were middle age White males and the rest of the class was composed of female students of color from diverse linguistic, ethnic, and social class backgrounds. One of the White male students tended to dominate the class discussion, and by doing so, he often silenced the female students of color. This White male student often behaved as if he knew it all about TESOL – having spent some time overseas teaching ESL (English as Second Language).

He came to my class with a banking concept of teaching as the late Brazilian educator Paulo Freire (1993) eloquently talked about in his book *Pedagogy of the Oppressed*. This student did not show much willingness to listen to and consider other point of views. He often interrupted his peers when expressed different views in class. Some of his peers came to me and complained about him. They stated that he made them feel uncomfortable with his disrespectful White male dominated behavior. It is worth reporting some of what the students said about this particular student. I changed everyone's name to protect their identity.

One of the students, a Latina woman, said,

> He is not a mature professional person because he constantly comments negatively about other peers. Another instance is that Jean (pseudonym) does not allow us as classmates to develop activities or dialogues. He is constantly interrupting and wanting to control all of the class discussions. He over criticizes other classmates presentations with negative feedback.

WHAT IT MEANS BEING BLACK IN THE IVY HALLS OF WHITE AMERICA   79

I invited the White male student to come to my office to talk to him about the complaint his peers made about him. He stated that he was not aware that his behavior and action made some of his peers feel uncomfortable. While talking to him about his peers' complaint, I made sure I treated him with respect that he deserved despite our different positions about race, class, gender, and diversity issues. I respectfully listened to him while he was explaining his side of the story. He was somewhat apologetic. He thanked me for bringing up to his attention how some of his peers felt about his behavior. However, his seemingly conservative views on issues such as diversity, language, race, and gender remained the same, as I will illustrate below using an accident that happened in class.

I invited Dr. Maria (pseudonym), a woman of color, to come to my class to talk about micro aggression. She began her talk using an example of linguistic discrimination she felt that she experienced as a graduate student while she was working with a professor. She stated that that professor made her feel stupid for not pronouncing an author's name the way the professor pronounced it. Specifically, she said that the professor laughed at her for not "properly" pronouncing the name Polluck. In her presentation, she also talked about an accident that occurred when she was invited to give her suggestion about a brochure her department was putting together to be distributed on campus. Once she realized that on the cover of the brochure there were only faces of Caucasian students, she suggested to her colleagues to include faces of people from diverse ethnic groups.

Her rationale for making such a suggestion was that she thought the cover page of the brochure did not reflect the student population of the university she was attending. A great majority of Hispanics and other ethnic groups were and still are attending that university. The student who was accused of making his female classmates of color uncomfortable in class vehemently reacted to her presentation. He posted a long message on blackboard for their peers to read. He reacted defensively in class and tried to dismiss what the guest speaker was saying. It is worth paraphrasing his reactions about the speaker's talk in order to illuminate the point that I aim to make here regarding his apparently racist behavior. He began his reaction by saying that the speaker's talk lacked substance and that her example of micro aggression and hostility were pathetic and ludicrous. He went further to say that some people have become too sensitive these days. He also said that he has been racially discriminated against as a White man. Specifically, he claimed that he was denied job that was offered to people of color who were not qualified. He added that Whites that are victims of this type of racial discrimination do not complain about it because they fear it is not politically correct to do so. He stated that the speaker's overreaction about her professor's comment on her pronunciation and accent was absurd and that she showed some level of ignorance for not trying to understand the background of the person who made the comment about the way she pronounced the word Polluck.

What is interesting is that it was only the two Caucasian White students out of 12 students of color taking that class who felt that the speaker's example of microagression was ludicrous and laughable. However, what the speaker shared in presentation was not laughable to the students of color. One of the female students of color reacted about the speaker's presentation as well as the reaction of the White male student stating:

> I realize and appreciate that school allows us the opportunity to express our opinions, but I do not appreciate it when it is at the expense of others. For example, when we had the guest speaker, Dr. Maria, I found Jean's actions to be unprofessional. I personally believe that a guest speaker should always be treated with the utmost respect despite if I agree with him or her. Dr. Maria presented an outstanding piece that empowered us; yet, the way that jean treated her did not value her as an individual – again, perpetuating the cycle of microagression.

That was not all. The following semester, the same individual student took a class with a colleague of mine. My colleague assigned to his students an article that I wrote about the presidency of Barack Obama. In this article, which was written right after President Obama was elected, I addressed important issues such as race, class, racism, and capitalism. I argued that it is unlikely that he would solve the racial and class issues awaiting him given that most of the people he appointed in his government are conservative privileged White males who have been benefiting from the U.S. political, racial, and socioeconomic system for decades and who, therefore, might not have any interest in helping President Obama to change such a system, if this was his agenda. In a required reaction to my article, instead of engaging the arguments or challenging the positions that I took in the article, this student went at great length to personally attack me accusing me of taking advantage of the U.S. government to immigrate here from a country destroyed by poverty and that now I have the audacity to talk against the U.S. capitalist system. What I have concluded from the erratic and apparently the racially motivated reaction of this White students is that perhaps he could not stand the fact that a Black man like me who, in his view, managed to escape oppressive government in my impoverished country, would call him on his sexist, reactionary, and racist attitude and actions in class and beyond. The painful experiences noted here have made

WHAT IT MEANS BEING BLACK IN THE IVY HALLS OF WHITE AMERICA   81

me question whether or not academia is a place where professors, particularly Black professors and other historically marginalized professors, might run the rick of losing their sanity, as a result of both systemic and individual racism. In the next section, I attempt to shed light on this issue drawing on my personal experience while situating such an experience in the larger racial and socio-historical context of the academia.

3   The Inner Fear of Losing Myself

After finishing my doctorate degree in 2008, I entered the academy with the hope of producing scholarly work that would positively influence the thoughts and minds of people, including those of younger generation. Such influence, so I hoped, would simultaneously inspire them to take actions aiming at making the world a little better than when they first entered it. Further, entering the academia as an educator, my goal was and continues to be to teach and prepare pre-service teachers, hoping they would become agents of social change in their teaching practices and beyond. In retrospect, I feel that I have accomplished such goals in some ways.

Some of my former students have already finished their degrees and have been teaching. For example, I visited the classroom of a former college student of mine, and I was happy to witness through classroom observation the progressive ideas that informed his teaching practices. Likewise, I have had people who randomly emailed me to tell me how much they have appreciated my scholarly work and they manner in which such a work has influenced their thoughts. Some have even contacted me requesting to interview me about some of my books, namely *Education under Occupation* and *The Agony of Masculinity*. As an example, Dr. Young Vershawn, host of *New Books in African American Studies* contacted me and requested an interview about *The Agony of Masculinity*.

Likewise, an Italian graduate student emailed me requesting an interview about my first book *Education under Occupation* after he had read it with the hope to gain further insights from me about the book, so he could incorporate them in his master's thesis. I have felt humbled by such emails and requests. Black Agenda Report recently contacted me for a set of interviews about my book on the former African American president, Barack Obama. The appreciation that random people have shown about my scholarly work has given the inner strength and inspiration to continue to write despite my busy schedule as a father of two children. Likewise the verbal appreciation and written thank you notes that former students of mine have expressed and sent to me about my teaching practices have inspired me to strive much more to become a better teacher every day.

In short, the reasons noted above have inspired me to stay in the academy despite countless ideological and racial wars I have had to battle against, including fighting colleagues who behave as chameleons. That is, colleagues that carry different changing colors and wear different hats to navigate through the system and move ahead at the expense of others. I do not feel that I can't ever trust these types of colleagues. Nonetheless, the acknowledgement that I have been fortunate to receive from random individuals about my work has helped me to maintain the enthusiasm and passion with which I entered the academy.

Looking back, I realize that I have been very naïve for trusting colleagues in the academy. This naivety derived from a lack of apprenticeship or proper training in graduate schools designed to adequately prepare young and recent graduates to enter academia, a milieu where internal ideological and racial wars often kill genuine passion, enthusiasm, and trusting attitude of many professors and students of color often leading to their cynicism. In the remainder of this chapter, I unravel these wars shaping the academic world. Specifically, drawing on direct observation and personal experiences as a Black professor, I analyze the ways and degree to which the oppressive and intoxicating parts of the academia might have caused the loss of some level of humanity in many professors, especially those who have been in the field for long time.

Exploring the root causes of some level of loss of humanity some professors have experienced is a daunting task, as there are many interwoven factors leading to such a loss. Like most institutions, universities and colleges, where professors teach and do research, are not free of oppression. In fact, many forms of oppression, such as racism, White supremacy, sexism, linguicism, ableism, and ageism have been occurring within these institutions more often than outsiders realize. Historically, heterosexual, abled-bodied, Christian, and conservative White males have dominated for the most part these institutions. With the exception of a few, women, Blacks, Latino/as, Native Americans, Asians, and other marginalized groups have been historically denied the opportunity to earn degrees, which would qualify them to enter these institutions. Thanks to the women, LGBTQ, and the civil right movements, colleges and universities have been compelled to open their doors to and create more spaces, though still limited, for women, including lesbian, bisexual, transgender women, and people of color whom these institutions tend to exclude.

As a Black professor, who was not born in this country, I have benefited from the hard work of those who were actively involved in these movements. Specifically, had it not been for the sacrifice of Rosa Park, Martin Luther, Malcom

WHAT IT MEANS BEING BLACK IN THE IVY HALLS OF WHITE AMERICA

X, and countless others, my life chances to have the opportunity to earn a doctorate degree and later become a university professor would have been limited, if not inexistent. For this reason, I deeply feel indebted to these freedom fighters.

However, such a privilege has not come without some heavy price, including psychological price. Though I have been in the academia for about 13 years, I have witnessed and, worse yet, have been a victim of the apparent loss of humanity of some colleagues. Such a loss seems to have been caused by the oppressive structure of the academic institution. For example, professors, particularly female professors, professors of color and queer professors, have faced racism, sexism, homophobia, and other forms of oppression at their institution. Likewise, progressive or dissident professors have often been isolated because of their ideology and positions against the conservative and corporate structure of many institutions. In addition, the hierarchical structure of many institutions has created the unequal power relations between those in power and those forcibly placed in subordinate positions. These forms of oppression have caused the loss of humanity in many professors.

The loss of humanity professors have experienced often leads them to mistreat their colleagues, particularly junior faculty, who are often forcibly placed in subaltern positions. Some professors have abused their senior status by trying to silence the voice of junior and associate faculty and blocking them from being granted tenure and promotion or full professorship. Sadly, historically marginalized groups are sometimes among the category of these oppressive professors. This is the sociological phenomenon that Paulo Freire (1993) and Frantz Fanon (1963) have eloquently talked about in their work. They argue that the oppressed, once liberated from their oppressive conditions, sometimes end up reproducing the same or similar forms of oppression by which they were once victimized. I have witnessed some of this occurring in the academia. Some senior faculty, including those of historically disfranchised groups, have oppressed other faculty by silencing their voice through professional meetings and, worse yet, conspiring against them so they would not get tenure and promotion or full professorship.

As noted earlier, such actions are caused by many underlying factors. The ideological and racial wars occurring at some departments or programs are often the root cause of discrimination and abuse against some faculty. Likewise, tension and conflicts stemming from competition, petit jealousy and envy have also led to unfair actions and decisions many senior faculty have taken against other faculty, particularly junior faculty. The source of such jealousy and envy is not hard to understand; some professors often feel threatened by their colleagues who are talented and prolific writers.

Big egos and empty rhetoric fly hard in the academic world leading to mistrust among many professors. From what I have observed, with the exception of a few cases, each professor seems to be doing his or her own things without showing much willingness, if any, to share with colleagues what projects he or she is working on, or contemplating, or he/she recently finished. Moreover, based on what I have witnessed many professors tend to be negative in their words and actions about their colleagues. This is due to the incredible competitive nature of academia. Apparently, some professors feel that they have to undermine or even ridicule other colleagues in order to make themselves appear better than anybody else. They perform intellectual competence like artists performing on stage at a theatre or in other settings. But through close observation, one can easily realize that it is all performance stripped of intellectual substance. Instead of encouraging colleagues, particularly junior faculty, who are thriving to succeed, some senior professors choose to psychologically wound and demoralize them with their harsh criticism and conspiracy. I personally have been victim of this form of micro-aggression by some senior faculty. While some have been overt in their aggressive and bullying tactics, others have been subtle. As previously noted, some have behaved like academic snakes that I do not feel I can ever trust.

Since entering the academia in fall 2008, I have been taken by the pressure of working like an intellectual maniac. To bluntly put it, I have been working like a machine that has thus far produced several peer-reviewed articles, books, and book chapters to feed the corporate-driven academic system. Because of internalized oppression, I feel that I have to work twice as hard as my Caucasian and native speakers colleagues in order to feel productive academically and earn the respect that I deserve as a scholar. To my dismay, however, I have learned through some trustworthy colleagues that my steady scholarly productivity has not been taken well by some senior faculty. In the words of those who confidentially shared with me the inside politics of my department and the college, my scholarly productivity has apparently caused jealousy and envy. Worse yet, I have been told, the unpleasant and negative comments some senior faculty have made about my academic performance, including my scholarship, might be informed by these factors. Because of my naivety and inclination to trust people's good heart, it took me about four years to finally believe what my colleagues shared with me about these senior faculty. Sometimes, I feel that I have been under their radar. As a result of this uncomfortable feeling, I have been trying to create my own academic sanctuary and strategically hide within it so as to maintain my sanity, protecting myself from academic violence often manifested in the form bullying and belittling.

WHAT IT MEANS BEING BLACK IN THE IVY HALLS OF WHITE AMERICA

My natural inclination to share with colleagues what I am working on in terms of research, book projects, and other kinds of projects precluded me from realizing sooner what some of my colleagues told me about the competitive and envious nature of academia. What has saddened me the most is that envious and competitive battles often occur among groups that have been all historically marginalized by the system. It seems to me some professors who have been oppressed but have managed to reach a certain level in the hierarchical power structure of the academia have in some way become oppressors of other historically marginalized professors. Institutional racism leading to many forms of internalized oppression, which many senior professors have developed, seems to be the root cause of such actions. These senior faculty seem to have lost some level of their humanity as a result of an institutional web of oppression to which they been subjected for decades. As an emerging scholar of color, I have already experienced the inner fear of losing some sense of my humanity, like many senior faculty of color, as a result of institutionalized oppression.

From what I have observed and witnessed, the loss of some level of humanity in some professors is often manifested through their cynical and authoritarian attitude and actions against colleagues, including junior faculty and students of color. Witnessing and being a victim of this has challenged me to start an introspective process trying to figure out whether I should dedicate the rest of my career in the academy. This process has prompted many questions, such as: Would I become miserable and cynical at some point in my career if I chose to stay in the academy? Should I try something different? If so, should I try to do so before or after earning tenure and promotion? Or should I stay in academia and try to be a role model for incoming junior faculty by genuinely and strongly supporting and mentoring them while at the same time continuing to produce high quality scholarship aiming to advance my field and beyond?

After self-reflection and introspection, I have come to the realization that the academic world is the one to which I feel I belong. I can't imagine myself doing something else, at least not now. Therefore, my challenges as a committed faculty of color are to find ways to maintain my humanity and sanity in an institution that historically has been unreceptive to people of African descent and other marginalized groups. I certainly do not want to become the cynical, the punitive, the envious, the miserable, and the authoritarian professor like many professors have become. To avoid becoming such a professor will be a terrific challenge, however. Part of the reason is that, as a Black professor, I have had already experienced many subtle and overt racially motivated strikes. Inevitably, throughout my academic journey, I will have many more racial wars and academic snakes to fight against. Nonetheless, as a person who is full of hope, life, enthusiasm, and endowed with a positive attitude, I will work hard to ensure that I do not ever lose some of sense of my humanity in the process of fighting these wars and snakes. Doing so will help me to avoid becoming the cynical, bitter, miserable, punitive, and gatekeeper types of professors that many colleagues, myself included, have to work with at some institutions.

4 Conclusion

As a Black man, I always feel the pressure to prove that I am intelligent, competent, a good person, and a good citizen, and that I am not irresponsible or aggressive – racially motivated constructs whose repercussions Blacks and other minority professors have to deal with. Despite incessant efforts to prove people wrong about the racial stereotypes about Black people that have been circulated in the mainstream media, especially in major Hollywood movies, I still have been victimized by racial prejudice. I have been paying a heavy price for simply being the offspring of African slaves. To simply put it, even before I was born, my racial fate was already configured by a structural racist world that has limited life chances of Blacks and many other marginalized groups. This racially constructed reality has caused me to feel that being born Black is being compelled to be ready early on in life to fight all forms of aggression in a world that is by and large cruel to people of African descent.

I sometimes wonder how my life would have been had I been born White with the same personality, ambition, and drive to succeed. My life would have been certainly different. Different in what way, one might ask? I do not know if I would be at the same position where I am now or at a higher position. But what I am certain of is that I will not have to constantly worry about my Black skin, which has increased my chance to be falsely accused of a crime that I do not commit, being unjustly shut by a racist police officer on the street, being denied housing and employment for which I am qualified, being denied access to quality healthcare, being forced to live in neighborhood where there are liquor stores on each street corner; where the air is polluted with chemical waste; in which there is lack of super market where I can buy healthy grocery, and where violence related to drug activities is rampant as a result of systemic inequality leading to abject poverty. This is not to suggest that I reject my blackness. In fact, my blackness is my redemption. Rather, what I am pointing here is the extent to which racism has impacted those who are dark. My social status as a professor has not, and will never protect from both individual and institutional racism, including racial profiling, racial fatigue, and micro aggression. Despite my friendly personality, work ethic, and professional success, I will always be victimized by structural racism unless we, people of color and White allies, collectively fight to eradicate it. I may not live long enough to witness this happen, but I do hope that my great, great grand-children will not just witness the eradication of racism but also take an active part in the grassroots movement leading to its end.

CHAPTER 8

The Cost of Being Black and Brown Laboring in Predominantly White Institutions

Racism feels like a scary shadow that follows Black and Brown people everywhere. What do I mean by that ? To illustrate and expand on this statement, I want to begin with the story of a famous professional Italian football player, Mario Balotelli, who played for the Liverpool football league. This famous Afro Italian football player, who was born to an immigrant Ghanaian family, was adopted as a child by an Italian Jew family and has faced various forms of discrimination, including being called monkey while playing soccer. Systemic racism follows Blacks and other people of color like a scary shadow in the U.S. academy, which feels, for many of us, like a race battlefield. Specifically, race and racism, among other pertinent factors, influence many decisions in the academy, including decisions about hiring and promoting faculty, administrators and staff.

I was naïve about the way in which race shapes the academy politically until I went through the tenure and promotion review process. The outcome of such review was a deep disappointment. In my judgment, it was full of exaggeration, inaccuracy, and unfairness coming from colleagues who claimed to be social justice educators, allies, and champions of diversity. Yet, they were cruelly vindictive, and racially biased in their verdict against my dossier. Like many minority professors, I gained a sound understanding of the racial biases embedded in the the tenure and promotion process when I started to participate in it. That is, I witnessed deceiving patterns and abuse of power perpetrated by senior colleagues in their vote deliberation and decisions against junior colleagues of color. Yet, they were the same colleagues who often used various forms of academic discourses colored with social justice, diversity, and equity propaganda to persuade others that they were socially just and "reliable" allies. As a prime example, at the previous institution where I taught, colleagues who pretended to be fiercely committed to, and champion of, social justice, were proven to be authoritarian, elitist, racist, xenophobic, and abusive in their behavior and actions against those who were in the lower scale of the academic hierarchy, including myself, as I have elaborated in the following narrative.

© KONINKLIJKE BRILL NV, LEIDEN, 2020 | DOI: 10.1163/9789004440944_009

THE COST OF BEING BLACK AND BROWN LABORING

1   Going through the Hoops of the Tenure and Promotion Process

As an assistant professor, the review of senior faculty always recommended my yearly dossier for tenure and promotion for five years consecutively. However, despite such performance, some colleagues viciously objected to my tenure and promotion application. Others, by contrast, who took part in the review process of my tenure and promotion dossier, stated that if they could, they would promote me to full professorship based on the following evidence of my professional performance (personal communication with two colleagues, November 2013 and April 2014, respectively).

At the previous institution where I taught for 9 years, I had published 12 peer review articles (11 solo and 1 co-authored) in respected journals, like *Journal of Black Studies*, while one was in press. I authored 8 books (7 solo and one co-authored); 6 edited and co-edited books; and 5 book chapters (4 solo and 1 co-authored) published by prestigious publishers, like Routledge and Palgrave. In addition, I received a 4.4/5 teaching average student performance accumulated over the course of five years. I was also granted two prestigious awards for scholarly productivity and accomplishments. Moreover, I successfully co-chaired and co-organized diversity lecture series on university campus in addition to serving on various college and university committees representing both the department and the designated program of which I was part. What is more, I successfully coordinated the program of which I was faculty member while at the same time chairing the Postcolonial and Education and Paulo Freire SIGs (special interest groups) at American Educational Research Association. Finally, in addition to service provided at the departmental, college, and university levels, I led workshops designed for teachers and administrators working with linguistically and culturally diverse students. This was part of an effort to build relationships with schools and communities.

Being aware of the unfair treatment that my tenure and promotion dossier application received at the departmental level, a colleague from a different department who participated in the review of such dossier at the college level asked of her partner, "What is wrong with your department, the Curriculum and Instruction department?" (personal communication with a colleague, March, 2014). My tenure and promotion application received unanimous supporting votes from colleagues participating in the review process at the college level, from the dean and the provost, whereas at the departmental level, it was unfairly treated. While this colleague's statement was emotionally uplifting at the time, such revelation indicated that my tenure and promotion application process was compromised. According to the stipulated rules in the official tenure and promotion document established by the former institution, the information about the outcome of my tenure and promotion review at the departmental level should have remained confidential.

The former department head at the time did not care enough to institutionally follow policy procedures to ensure that my tenure and promotion application was fairly treated. She carelessly allowed colleagues reviewing my tenure and promotion dossier at the college level to have access to both the letter she wrote and the letter the chair of the tenure and promotion committee at the departmental level wrote on my behalf – a violation of the tenure and promotion procedure. In my humble opinion, both letters were full of premeditated biases, unfairness, and inequity, and thus lack of professional integrity – expression routinely used and preached by the very same group of colleagues who participated in the institutional coup against my tenure and promotion dossier.

They ensured that colleagues participating in the tenure and promotion review process at the college level had access to the letters that both from the former department head and the tenure and promotion committees wrote about my dossier. Making these letters accessible to colleagues at the college level was part of the plan to influence the decision about my dossier since the two letters of recommendation at departmental level were plagued with biases. Simply stated, this department head and her co-conspirators wanted both her biased letter and that of the tenure and promotion committee to influence the outcome of the votes of colleagues at the college level about my tenure and promotion. It was not a coincidence that the former department head and her co-conspirators plotted against my tenure and promotion dossier given their long standing passive but aggressive attitude, behavior, and actions toward me and other minority professors and students who did not go by their authoritarian rules.

According to the tenure and promotion document at the previous institution, department heads were expected to adequately guide faculty submitting their dossier for tenure and promotion review. However, the former department head, whose responsibility was to guide me through such process, failed to do so. Before I submitted my tenure and promotion portfolio, I reached out to her, and we met only once for about two hours. While we were meeting, she provided feedback mostly on the esthetic aspect of the portfolio. I asked her if she would be willing to look at the portfolio once more before I submitted it for review to the tenure and promotion committee made of some senior faculty, including people of color, who had earned the reputation of being gatekeepers. She declined my request saying "You can have somebody else look at it for you." She then abruptly got up, and returned to her desk moving on with her own business. I left her office feeling emotionally and professionally hurt.

This was the last meeting we had before I turned in my tenure and promotion documents for review. Frustrated for not having a mentor at the department who could have guided me at the time and feeling poorly treated by an unsupportive department head, I wanted to postpone my application for tenure and promotion. However, I did not. I instead dig into my inner self to find spiritual force, so that I would not allow the former department head alongside her co-conspirators to deter me from stepping forward.

I applied for tenure and promotion despite the lack of support, including from the department head and my assigned mentor. The senior faculty who was assigned to be my mentor as an assistant professor was warm, friendly, and welcoming, particularly when my family and I first arrived there. However, with regard to mentorship, he did very little, if anything. He once said to the first former department head – a fine colleague and administrator – that "Pierre doesn't need a mentor (with a phony smile)." Imagine being on your first year as an assistant professor and you have a full/distinguished professor assigned to you as your mentor saying to you in front of your department head that you're fine and that you do not need a mentor! I felt a lack of care in such statement.

He acted on it throughout my time there, for he did not seem to care whether I succeeded or not. In fact, I was told that he was part of the conspiracy against my tenure and promotion dossier. He did not show up to participate in the voting process supposedly because he was out of town. But his closest ally, colleague, and very good friend, who was one of the meanest, abusive, and egocentric colleagues, took part in the discussion and decision-making sure his voice was represented through the processes of my tenure and promotion. One can imagine the rest!

My experiences with this process were nothing but an ordeal until I received the final letter in April 2014 confirming that I was granted tenure and promotion. What do I mean by this statement? While waiting on the outcome of the review of my dossier, some information leaked indicating that such review was atrociously unfair to the point where some close colleagues advised me to consider to start looking for jobs elsewhere even before I received the official letter. They were concerned that I might be denied tenure and promotion based on what they knew but could not reveal for ethical and professional reasons. I refuted such advice, as I remained convinced that colleagues at the college level, external reviewers, the dean of the college, the associate dean, and the provost will see the value of my dossier and they will support it. They did, indeed, support it. I earned tenure and promotion despite the conspiracy of some colleagues against my dossier at departmental level. However, the aftermath of such experience lingers and has shaped my outlook on the academy.

Specifically, this experience has made realize that the academy is not an easy terrain for minority professors with integrity and dignity to navigate, as they constantly face micro-aggressions, including academicism, from other minorities. Navigating the academy requires understanding first and foremost its elite culture, which shapes its political nature.

Joining the senior faculty club appeared to have been one of the underlying reasons explaining the fruitless attempt of some prejudiced and elitist senior faculty to gate keep assistant professors from being promoted to associate or full professor. Their conspiracy has left a psychological scar in me, particularly as some colleagues that I trusted allied with two known racist and xenophobic colleagues in the department to plot against my dossier. People of color experience psychological scar in various *contexts*. In the western academy, they are often bullied, undermined, underestimated, and dis-respected by racially prejudiced students and colleagues, as well as by other minority colleagues who are very elitist and classist in their behavior and actions.

Minority groups are often questioned about their intelligence and qualification for positions they are qualified and sometimes overqualified. They are so very often labeled arrogant, angry or agitated because of their assertiveness and self-confidence. For instance, the former department head that I referred to earlier stated once that I got agitated when I spoke. Specifically, while we were meeting, I asked the former department head about her assessment of me as an assistant professor. Instead of talking about and focusing on my professional performance, she jumped to label me by saying: "You tend to get a little bit agitated when you speak." She went on to say, "Before I got to know you, I thought you were arrogant; now, I don't necessarily think so." She failed to understand moving my body while speaking is how I culturally I communicate. That is, I use body language while speaking. Instead of making an effort to ask why I moved my arms and face a lot when I spoke, she conveniently placed me in a racial box.

Professors of color have also been called names, like nigger or bitch (in the case of female professors of color). Additionally, they are often underpaid and yet expected to overwork to meet institutional expectations and needs. Furthermore, they are habitually denied promotions opportunities at a much higher rate than their White counterparts even though quantitatively and statistically they are the minority in the academy (Orelus, 2018). Lastly, White conservative colleagues often discriminate against professors of color in ways that might not have been intended to be discriminatory. Nonetheless, it still hurts.

Like structural racism, abuse of status by some colleagues often make assistant and even associate professors feel uneasy and unsafe within the U.S. ivory tower. As a first generation university professor of color, I often feel that I am climbing a mountain full of emotional hurdles within the U.S. ivory tower shaped by envious, racist, elitist, and xenophobic colleagues who have tried to treat me as a subaltern regardless of my tenured status and rank. My first year as a Black assistant professor was very challenging. I was very naïve and unaware of double standards, unspoken expectations, deceits, back stabbings, and hypocrisy that shaped the culture of the department where I worked and the academy as a whole. I would talk to colleagues about manuscripts I was working on, only to discover later that these colleagues were very insecure, envious, jealous, and elitist.

During my third year, I more or less understood the codes regimenting the U.S. academy, including unspoken rules and expectations set for certain groups of faculty, particularly faculty of color and female faculty. These faculty members over served only to be told through their yearly review that they would not obtain tenure and promotion if they did not publish – even though they were hard pressed to over serve and consequently did not have sufficient quality time and mental space to write and publish. Before I left, two female faculty of color were denied promotion, while one was granted tenure. One of them ended up leaving that institution and went back to her native land, Puerto Rico, as she could no longer bear the unfairness. Some tenured faculty were forced to transfer to another department within the same university, while another full professor of color, who was a great mentor to me while I was there, decided to retire earlier than planned in order to keep her human dignity in tact.

Lacking awareness early one in my career as a university professor precluded me from understanding ways and the degree to which, for example, institutional elitism, racism, jealousy, envy, rivalry, and xenophobia influence yearly review and the tenure and promotion process and outcomes particularly for faculty of color. Toward the end of my 5th year as an assistant professor, I gained a sound understanding of the academy. I uncovered deceiving patterns in many colleagues' behavior and actions. Specifically, I was able to reveal the hypocrisy, the unfairness, and the abuse of status by some colleagues in the higher scale of the academic hierarchy. These individuals often adopted the social justice dominant discourse to persuade others that they were socially just. Yet, they were among the most unfair and abusive colleagues. In the academy those placed in lower scale of the elitist hierarchy, including students, assistant professors of color, and female professors, are often victims of social injustices committed by those holding higher positions. Hierarchy perpetuates oppression by favoring those in powerful positions, while marginalizing the powerless or the least powerful. Hierarchy often gives those in power the illusion that they are superior to, more powerful and smarter than, those in lower hierarchical positions. As a result, many often mistreat and oppress people they perceive as being less and lower than them. Ego, insecurity, and envy have caused many people, including self-declared champions and defenders of social justice, to mistreat and oppress others leading to *psychological scar*.

Through my professional journey, I have known many self-declared social justice educators, who are elitist, abusive, and are not trust-worthy individuals. In my experiences working with them, I have found them to be insecure, condescending, unfair, and oppressive to others. Yet, they often use the grand social justice discourse to make people believe that they are unbiased and fair. Through this discourse, many sound like the champion and defender of social justice, even though they are self-serving, dishonest, and unfair. Sadly, many have been successful at doing so – sometimes for years before the veil of their pseudo social justice discourse falls and exposes itself. My personal experiences with racist, elitist, authoritarian, xenophobic, and envious colleagues have led me to question the social justice discourse circulating in the academy.

2 Post-Tenure and Promotion Critical Self-Reflection

Few months after I was promoted to associate professor position at my past institution, I took a year sabbatical leave. While I was on sabbatical, I had time to reflect on my professional trajectory, including my tenure and promotion experiences. While reflecting on these experiences, I took into account the privilege that comes with being tenured and promoted. For example, because I am tenured, I was able to take a year off to finish a couple of projects while continuing to work with doctoral students, to spend quality time with my family, close friends, and neighbors, and to take better care of myself. Also, I had the opportunity to further explore my culture and network with professionals working in the field of education in my native land.

Finally, the year sabbatical enabled me to deeply reflect on my professional experiences, both positive and disappointing. In critically reflecting on these experiences, I have become keenly aware of the elitist, unfair, biased, and hypocritical nature of the western academy, which has paradoxically allowed me to prepare students, including prospective teachers, to serve humanity. During my tenure at my past institution, I had the privilege to teach and mentor the best minds in the South West. Most of my students were of Mexican descent and working class Whites. My experience working with them was nothing but remarkable. I am still in touch with some of my mentees. Upon graduation, some of them went on to teach, while others went law school and have been practicing laws.

Since I have become a university professor, I have witnessed the constant fight among colleagues for social status, public recognition, and fame. At the

THE COST OF BEING BLACK AND BROWN LABORING   95

same time, I have had the opportunity to know colleagues, including White colleagues, who walk the talk. That is, they match social justice theories to their behavior and actions. I have not been disappointed with these colleagues. They do not preach on social justice, fairness, and equity issues. Instead, they have lived and embodied them in their daily praxis. I call these colleagues and scholars social justice praxiers (Orelus, 2017).

In the academic universe, tenure is considered a lifetime job. To my knowledge, no professor has been stripped of his or her tenure, except in rare cases where the professor violates university policy implicating in selling or consuming illegal drugs on campus, being accused and found guilty of sexual harassment, or being involved in physical fights with students and found to be at fault, among other exceptional cases. Indeed, being tenured is unquestionably a golden privilege one can ever have. This does not suggest, however, that all tenured professors enjoy such privilege the same way or to the same extent. Race, gender, class, sexuality, language, nationality, and religion, among other variables, determine who gets to benefit more from tenure and promotion privileges and opportunities than others.

These variables shape, for example, unequal power relations between professors of color and White professors; female and male professors; queer and non-queer professors; and domestic and immigrant professors. Not all tenured and promoted professors feel happy and celebrate their tenure and promotion, even though being tenured remains a privilege in itself; it provides job security and some degree of mental peace with regard of being unfairly terminated. Tenured professors can't just be terminated, as this often leads to lawsuits. Some have used their privileged status as tenured faculty to denounce abusive and unfair practices taking place in the academy – something some faculty might be afraid of doing prior to being tenured.

There are those who choose to remain complicit with the system, regardless of whether or not they are tenured. Finally, one finds those who have been radical throughout their professional career. They are a minority, and they often suffer tremendously within the U.S. academy. Earning tenure and promotion automatically puts me in a safer position in the academy to continue to inspire and prepare students for challenges awaiting them beyond the ivory tower. In terms of status, earning tenure and promotion places me in a different location in the academic hierarchy. I am now part of the senior faculty exclusive club. Being part of this elitist club has its own challenges and responsibilities. At my previous institution, I got to sit at the same table together with senior colleagues who did not want me to be there in the first place. Some of whom welcome me back from sabbatical with a phony and nervous smile saying, "Pierre, welcome back! How was the sabbatical?" as if they missed me. This is a perfect example of hypocrisy hidden through smiling faces. Further, by virtue of being tenured and promoted, I am allowed to participate in the review of assistant professors' yearly performance as well as tenure and promotion dossier.

This privileged position has enabled me to bear witness to many cases of double standards, abuse of status by senior faculty, partiality, hypocrisy, and unfairness.

For example, at my previous institution, I observed some senior faculty harshly criticizing the portfolio of some competent, talented, highly qualified, and confident faculty of color that they did not seem to like. They seemed to base their judgment on their perception of the faculty's personality, great ambition, aspiration, and personal and professional choices. They used arguments, like "he/she is not doing what we ask him/her to do," as if these junior faculty were rebellious children that needed to be tamed, for they refused to obey their orders. Also, there were cases of surveillance of some faculty who are prolific and dared collaborate with colleagues outside their institution that some senior faculty did not seem to approve of. I was one of the assistant professors, who was subjected to this type of surveillance. I have been supported by, and have collaborated with, many respected scholars in my respective field and beyond. Once, while hurrying to go teach my evening class, I overheard two senior faculty talking about me. Referring to me, one of them said "what can't he collaborate with us here? Why does he have to collaborate with Peter McLaren and Noam Chomsky?" The other responded, "I think he is kissing their ass."

The two colleagues that these senior professors named in their conversation, and with whom I indeed collaborated, have been very supportive to me and have continued to inspire me to be a prolific writer and scholar activist. I observed some of my former colleagues trying their hardest at meetings to defend the dossier of their protégées who were, in my experience working with them, average scholars. They supported colleagues who were submissive and willing to bow to them. They voted against colleagues they did not like; while voting, they made unpleasant statements about their scholarship, teaching, and character, in a vicious attempt to destroy their reputation. At my previous institution, I witnessed and personally experienced injustices, biases, and unfairness committed by so-called social justice educators.

3   Looking Forward

I might not fully understand the way western society, including the academy, functions, in terms of who runs it; what ideology that shapes its culture and practices; who gets to stay in power and promoted; who gets pushed in or out; who gets stuck in the same position because of their race, gender, sexuality,

THE COST OF BEING BLACK AND BROWN LABORING   97

language or accent; whose work is valued, and which one is often undermined; who gets to speak on behalf of whom; who are the real social justice praxiers (Orelus, 2017), and who are the hypocrite ones; who are the caring, loving, and knowledgeable educators and who are the oppressive ones and great performers; who gets to decide on behalf of whom; and, finally, whose ideology and actions challenge the status quo and which ones that serve to maintain it. Therefore, I might not know the answers to these problematic situations and how to solve them all. However, based on my experiences as a Black professor, father, and family man, I have learned that one needs to focus on:

– Taking better care one's self, spiritually, emotionally, and physically besides doing so professionally and intellectually
– Teaching in a smarter way than before while continuing to care for, support, and mentor students
– Doing research on, and writing about, what one feels really passionate about
– Collaborating with fair, trustworthy, reliable, and respectful colleagues from all backgrounds and institutions and disciplines who value valuable work
– Being involved more in communities beyond the ivory tower
– Participating in committees that are meaningful, that is, conducive to one's intellectual and professional growth
– Staying away from untrustworthy, hypocritical, envious, condescending, egocentric, oppressive, and negative colleagues. Keep it only collegial and polite with them!
– Trusting one's self first more, and then those who have earned one's trust.
– Being more cautious with liberal, progressive, or even radical people in their grand discourses, without any exception, since performance is not essence and appearance is not substance.
– Being compassionate and forgiving to people, including those who have racially discriminated against me, for I am keenly aware that many of us have been brainwashed since childhood, and have not had transcended or unlearned what we were taught as a child or adolescent. As a result, we hold prejudice and even hatred against other people who might have nothing against us.

Afterword

In a white world that demands that the black body surrender itself to the indignities of racism and de facto segregation, Pierre Orelus is a voice that needs to be urgently heard. Shaken by the trauma of poverty while growing up a rawboned youth in the Haitian countryside where his mother survived by shouldering heavy sacks of rice, beans, sugar, and salt, and where his family had no access to running water, electricity, telephone, or television, Orelus became awakened to one of the major contradictory faultlines of living in a capitalist society: the ugliness of class oppression and the richness of his family and his cultural heritage. Defying great odds, Orelus was able to attend college and move to the United States where he worked alongside other immigrants washing dishes and cleaning floors in nursing homes, shopping malls, and hotels.

Moving from a country where communities are actually segregated by class to a white world that is structurally segregated by race and by class, was another rude awakening which Orelus described as living in the shadows.

While living in the shadows, and with the help of the critical works of Frantz Fanon, Albert Memmi, Paulo Freire and others, Orelus not only learned to reflect upon how much the Haitian school system was a prisoner of its own coloniality of power, but he aimed his newly minted critical skills at the academy of which he had become a part. This became part of a cycle that Orelus refers to as his all encompassing "ontological struggle" so powerfully rendered in these pages in which the author is brutally honest about his struggle to transcend his own unearned privileges – for instance, as straight Black man who worked hard to overcome his heterosexual normativity – while at the same time being buried under the folie à groupe of white authority.

Yet looming from these shadows is a splinter of light that is the hope seized upon by Orelus as he deeply considers the richness of Black America and its long collective struggle for freedom. And the struggles of Black people from the Middle Passage to Black diasporas throughout the world. He carries this insight into the ivy halls of white America, all the while shouldering the consequences of the reciprocally generative nature of racism and capitalism that has not spared professors of color by any stretch of the imagination. Orelus' own story, of a child seemingly entombed in a life of poverty, reaching the shores of the American dream with the loving help and sacrifices of his relatives only to learn what consequences await a Black man who dares to reach for American dream, often means having to stare constantly into the heart of white supremacy, navigating a warren of possibilities, all tainted by capitalism and its twin

© PETER MCLAREN, 2020 | DOI: 10.1163/9789004440944_010

horror, racism, and threatening at any moment to ensepulcher him in a gran-ite-cut chamber filled with white terror. This is a book that must be read, and read again and again.

Peter McLaren
Distinguished Professor in Critical Studies
Chapman University

References

Acuña, R. (2008). *Corridors of migration: The Odyssey of Mexican laborers, 1600–1933*. University of Arizona Press.

Acuña, R. (2010). *Occupied America: A history of Chicanos* (7th ed.). Prentice Hall.

Ahmed, S. (2000). *Strange encounters: Embodied others in post-coloniality*. Routledge.

Aldama, A. (2001). *Disrupting savagism: Intersecting Chicana/o, Mexican immigrant, and Native American struggles for self-representation*. Duke University Press.

Anzaldua, G. (2007). *Borderlands/La frontera: The new mestiza* (3rd ed.). Aunt Lute Books.

Appiah, K. A. (2005). *The ethics of identity*. Princeton University Press.

Bell, D. (1992). *Faces at the bottom of the well: The permanence of racism*. Basic Books.

Bell, D. (2009). Who's afraid of critical race theory? In E. Taylor, D. Gillborn, & G. Ladson-Billings (Eds.), *Foundations of critical race theory in education* (pp. 37–50). Routledge.

Bell, L. A. (2010). *Storytelling for social justice: Connecting narrative and the arts in antiracist teaching*. Routledge.

Bhabha, H. (1994). *The location of culture*. Routledge.

Bloom, A. (1989). *The closing of the American mind*. Simon & Schuster.

Blumenfeld, W. J. (2006). Christian privilege and the promotion of "secular" and not-so "secular" mainline Christianity in public schooling and in the larger society. *Equity & Excellence in Education, 3*, 195–210.

Bonilla-Silva, E. (2010). *Anything but racism: How social scientists limit the significance of race*. Routledge.

Bonilla-Silva, E. (2018). *Racism without racists: Color-blind racism and the persistence of racial inequality in the United States*. Rowman & Littlefield. (Original work published 2003)

Bourdieu, P. (1986). The forms of capital. In J. G. Richardson (Ed.), *Handbook of theory and research for the sociology of education* (pp. 240–260). Greenwood.

Bourdieu, P. (1990). *The logic of practice* (R. Nice, Trans.). Stanford University Press.

Bourdieu, P. (1991). *Language and symbolic power* (G. Raymond & M. Adamso, Trans.). Polity.

Bourdieu, P. (1998). *Practical reason*. Polity.

Brown, M., Carnoy, M., Currie, E., Duster, T., Oppenheimer, D., Shultz, M., & Wellman, D. (2003). *Whitewashing race: The myth of a color-blind society*. University of California Press.

Buchanan, P. (2004). *Where the right went wrong: How neoconservatives subverted the Reagan revolution and hijacked the Bush presidency*. Thomas Dunne Books.

Butler, J. P. (2009). *Giving an account of oneself*. Fordham University Press.

Cabral, A. (1973). *Return to the source: Selected speeches by Amílcar Cabral.* Monthly Review Press.

Castells, M. (2006). *The power of identity* (Vol. 2, 2nd ed.). Blackwell.

Chomsky, N. (1994). *Secrets, lies and democracy.* Odonian Press.

Chomsky, N. (2002a). *Media control: The spectacular achievements of propaganda.* Seven Stories Press.

Chomsky, N. (2002b). *Understanding power: The indispensable Chomsky.* New Press.

Chomsky, N. (2004). *Hegemony or survival: America's quest for global dominance.* Holt Paperbacks.

Chomsky, N., Goodman, A., Famer, P., Aristide, J. B., & Aristide, M. (2004). *Getting Haiti right this time: The U.S. and the coup.* Common Courage Press.

Collins, P. H. (1998). *Fighting words: Black women and the search for justice.* Routledge.

Coloma, R. S. (2008). Border crossing subjectivities and research: Through the prism of feminists of color. *Race Ethnicity and Education, 11*(1), 11–27.

Dalmage, H. M. (2002). *Tripping on the color line: Black-White multiracial families in a racially divided world.* Rutgers University Press.

Danticat, E. (1996). *Krik? Krak!* Vintage.

Danticat, E. (1998). *Breath, eyes and memory.* Vintage.

Delgado, R. (1989). Storytelling for oppositionists and others: A plea for narrative. *Michigan Law Review, 87,* 2411–2441.

Delgado, R., & Stefancic, J. (1995). *Critical race theory: The cutting edge.* Temple University Press.

De Tocqueville, A., & Grant, S. (2000). *Democracy in America.* Hackett.

Dewey, J. (1997). *Democracy and education.* Free Press.

Du Bois, W. E. B. (1995). *The souls of Black folk.* Penguin.

Dupuy, A. (1989). *Haiti in the world economy: Class, race, and underdevelopment since 1700.* Westview Press.

Dupuy, A. (2006). *The prophet and power: Jean-Bertrand Aristide, the international community, and Haiti.* Rowman & Littlefield.

Ellison, R. (1980). *The invisible man.* [Kindle edition]. Retrieved from Amazon.com

Espín, O. (1997). *Latina realities: Essays on healing, migration, and sexuality.* Westview Press.

Fanon, F. (1963). *The wretched of the earth.* Grove Press.

Fanon, F. (1965). *A dying colonialism.* Grove Press.

Fanon, F. (1967). *Black skin, White masks.* Grove Press.

Farmer, P. (2003). *The uses of Haiti.* Common Courage Press.

Feagin, J. R. (2006). *Systemic racism: A theory of oppression.* Routledge.

Foucault, M. (1995). *Discipline and punish: The birth of the prison* (A. Sheridan, Trans.). Vintage Books.

Freire, P. (1993). *Pedagogy of the oppressed* (M. Ramos, Trans.). Continuum. (Original work published 1970)

REFERENCES

Freire, P., & Macedo, D. (1987). *Literacy: Reading the word and the world*. Bergin & Garvey.

Gillborn, D. (2005). Education as an act of White supremacy: Whiteness, critical race theory and education reform. *Journal of Education Policy, 20*(4), 485–505.

Gillborn, D. (2008). *Racism and education: Coincidence or conspiracy?* Routledge.

Grande, S. (2004). *Red pedagogy: Native American social and political thought*. Rowman & Littlefield.

Hirsch Jr., E. D. (1987). *Cultural literacy: What every American needs to know*. Vintage.

Holland, D. (2003). *Identity and agency in cultural worlds*. Harvard University Press.

Jensen, B. (2004). *The heart of Whiteness: Confronting race, racism, and White privilege*. City Lights Books.

hooks, b. (1984). *Feminist theory: From margin to center*. South End Press.

hooks, b. (1989). *Talking back: Thinking feminist, thinking Black*. South End Press.

Kozol, J. (1986). *Illiterate America*. Anchor Press/Doubleday.

Kozol, J. (1992). *Savage inequalities: Children in America's schools*. Crown.

Ladson-Billings, G. (2004). Just what is critical race theory and what's it doing in a nice field like education? In G. Ladson-Billings & D. Gillborn (Eds.), *The Routledge Falmer reader in multicultural education* (pp. 49–264). Routledge Falmer.

Leonardo, Z. (2005). *Critical pedagogy and race*. Wiley Blackwell.

Leonardo, Z. (2009). *Race, Whiteness, and education*. Routledge.

Leonardo, Z. (2011). Unmasking White supremacy and racism: A conversation with Zeus Leonardo. In P. Orelus (Ed.), *Rethinking race, class, language, and gender: A dialogue with Noam Chomsky and other leading scholars*. Rowman & Littlefield.

Lynn, M., Riser, C., & Yeigh, M. (2018). An intergenerational conversation between Dr. Marvin Lynn and Chris Riser: Social activism and the Black male educator. *Northwest Journal of Teacher Education, 13*(2), 5.

Macedo, D. (1994). *Literacies of power: What Americans are not allowed to know*. Westview Press.

Macedo, D., Dendrinos, B., & Gounari, P. (2003). *The hegemony of English*. Paradigm.

Marable, M. (2002). *The great wells of democracy: The meaning of race in American life*. Basic Civitas Books.

Massey, D., & Denton, N. (1993). *American apartheid*. Harvard University Press.

Matsuda, M. J., Lawrence, C., Delgado, R., & Crenshaw, K. W. (1993). *Words that wound: Critical race theory, assaultive speech, and the first amendment*. Westview Press.

Mayo, P. (2017). Gramsci, hegemony and educational politics. In N. Pizzolato & J. D. Holst (Eds.), *Antonio Gramsci: A pedagogy to change the world* (pp. 35–47). Springer.

McIntosh, P. (1992). White privilege and male privilege: A personal account to see correspondences through work in women's studies. In M. Anderson & P. H. Collins (Eds.), *Race, class, and gender: An anthology* (pp. 70–81). Wadsworth.

Memmi, A. (1965). *The colonizer and the colonized*. Beacon Press.

Mills, C. (1999). *The racial contract*. Cornell University Press.

Mohanty, C. (2003). "Under western eyes" revisited: Feminist solidarity through anticapitalist struggles. In C. Mohanty (Ed.), *Feminism without borders: Decolonizing theory, practicing solidarity*. Duke University Press.

Montero-Sieburth, M. (2000). The use of cultural resilience in overcoming contradictory encounters in academia: A personal narrative. In E. H. Trueba & L. Bartolome (Eds.), *Immigrant voices: In search of educational equity* (pp. 218–245). Rowman & Littlefield.

Morrell, E. (2015). Toward a critical pedagogy of race: Ethnic studies and literacies of power in high school classrooms. *Race and Social Problems, 7*(1), 84–96.

Morrell, E. (2018). *Educating Harlem: Schooling and resistance in an American Community*. Columbia University Press.

Myrdal, G. (1944). *An American dilemma: The Negro problem and modern democracy*. Harper & Brothers.

Nieto, S. (2002). *Language, culture, and teaching: Critical perspectives for a new century*. Lawrence Erlbaum Associates.

Noguera, P. (2008). *The trouble with Black boys: ... and other reflections of race, equity, and the future of public education*. John Wiley.

Norton, B. (2000). *Identity and language learning: Gender, ethnicity, and educational change*. Longman.

Omi, M., & Winant, H. (1994). *Racial formation in the United States: From the 1960s to the 1980s*. Routledge.

Orelus, P. W. (2007). *Education under occupation: The heavy price of living in a neocolonized and globalized world*. Sense Publishers.

Orelus, P. W. (2009). *The agony of masculinity: Race, gender, and education in the age of "new" racism and patriarchy*. Peter Lang.

Orelus, P. W. (2011). *Rethinking race, class, language, and gender: A dialogue with Noam Chomsky and other leading scholars*. Rowman & Littlefield.

Orelus, P. W. (2018). Can subaltern professors speak? Examining micro-aggressions and lack of inclusion in the academy. *Qualitative Research Journal, 18*(2), 169–179.

Pennycook, A. (2001). *English and the discourses of colonialism*. Routledge.

Phillipson, R. (1992). *Linguistic imperialism*. Oxford University Press.

Ravitch, D. (1990). Diversity and democracy: Multicultural education in America. *American Educator, 14*(1), 16–20, 46–68.

Richardson, L. (2000). Writing: A method of inquiry. In N. Denzin & Y. Lincoln (Eds.), *The Sage handbook of qualitative research*. Sage.

Said, E. (1978). *Orientalism*. Vintage.

Said, E. (1996). *Representations of the intellectuals*. Vintage Books.

Said, E. (2000). *Reflections on exile and other essays*. Harvard University Press.

Schneider, A. (1998). What has happened to faculty diversity in California? *Chronicle of Higher Education, 45*(13), A9–A12.

REFERENCES

Smith, L. T. (1999). *Decolonizing methodologies: Research and indigenous people.* Zed Books.

Spivak, G. (1988). Can the subaltern speak? In C. Nelson & L. Grossberg (Eds.), *Marxism and the interpretation of culture.* University of Illinois Press.

Stovall, D. (2006, September). Forging community in race and class: Critical race and the quest for social justice in education. *Race, Ethnicity, and Education, 9*(3), 243–259.

Subreenduth, S. (2008, March). Deconstructing the politics of a differently colored transnational identity. *Race Ethnicity and Education, 11*(1), 41–55.

Thiong'o, N. (1986). *Decolonizing the mind: The politics of language in African literature.* Heinemann.

Torres, M. (2004). To the margins and back: The high cost of being Latina in America. *Journal of Latinos and Education, 3*(2), 123–141.

Trouillot, M. R. (1995). *Silencing the past: Power and the production of history.* Beacon Press.

West, C. (1993). *Race matters.* Beacon Press.

West, C. (2004). *Democracy matters: Winning the fight against imperialism.* Penguin Press.

Yosso, T. J., Smith, W. A., Ceja, M., & Solórzano, D. G. (2009). Critical race theory, racial microaggressions, and campus racial climate for Latina/o undergraduates. *Harvard Educational Review, 79*(4), 659–690.

Zinn, H. (2003). *A people's history of the United States.* Harper & Row.

Printed in the United States
By Bookmasters